# COMMON SENSE
# IN CHESS

# COMMON SENSE
# IN CHESS

## by Emanuel Lasker

Corrected by David A. Mitchell

New York
DOVER PUBLICATIONS, INC.

*Library of Congress Catalog Card Number: 65-20485*

Manufactured in the United States of America

Dover Publications, Inc.
180 Varick Street
New York 14, N.Y.

# PREFACE

THE following is an abstract of Twelve Lectures given before an audience of London chess players during the spring of 1895. It may be regarded as an attempt to deal with all parts of a game of chess by the aid of general principles. The principles laid down are deduced from considerations concerning the nature of Chess as a fight between two brains, and their conception is based on simple facts. Their practical working has been illustrated by positions adapted to the purpose, and likely to occur over the board.

It has been my aim to reduce the different rules in number as much as was compatible with clearness. They all, it will be found, have a remote likeness, and it would therefore not have been very difficult to reduce their number still more. Indeed, they may ultimately be united in one single leading principle, which is the germ of the theory not only of Chess, but of any kind of fight. This principle is sufficiently indicated here, but it is so general in its conception, and the difficulty of expressing the whole compass of its meaning in definite terms so enormous, that I have not ventured to formulate it. In a future work, for which the present one shall pave the way, I hope to be able to illustrate the significance of that principle, and its capacity for showing facts in their right relation to one another. For that work I have also deferred the discussion of some points which

7

require very nice differentiation, such as all questions relating to the manœuvring of the King and the exchange of men.

The games and positions given in this book are comparatively few, but they have been selected with care. I therefore would advise the student not to attempt to *read* the matter only, but to *study* it and sink some work into it. The rules deduced are, I believe, very plausible. This need not deceive the student, who will see their significance in a clearer light if he tries to be reasonably skeptical and exacting in the matter of proofs.

As regards the analytical notes about games or openings, I have tried to be short and to the point. Analytical detail is therefore not abundant, but, I think, reliable. The method of enumerating *all* the variations thought possible, or probable, has been laid aside, and in its place an analysis has been given, which makes use of both the consideration of the leading variations *and* general principles. The diction and style of the work are those of a lecturer. Feeling that I have not been able to make them as perfect as I should have desired, I must ask for the lenient judgment of the reader.

I take this opportunity for expressing my hearty thanks to Professor Villin Marmery for his kind assistance in looking over the proofs.

EMANUEL LASKER.

# COMMON SENSE
## IN CHESS

# COMMON SENSE IN CHESS

## No. 1

Gentlemen: It is customary to begin with definitions, but I am sure that all of you are so well acquainted with the essential parts of the history, the rules and the characteristics of Chess, that you will allow me to jump at once *in medias res*. Chess has been represented, or shall I say misrepresented, as a game—that is, a thing which could not well serve a serious purpose, solely created for the enjoyment of an empty hour. If it were a game only, Chess would never have survived the serious trials to which it has, during the long time of its existence, been often subjected. By some ardent enthusiasts Chess has been elevated into a science or an art. It is neither; but its principal characteristic seems to be—what human nature mostly delights in—a fight. Not a fight, indeed, such as would tickle the nerves of coarser natures, where blood flows and the blows delivered leave their visible traces on the bodies of the combatants, but a fight in which the scientific, the artistic, the purely intellectual element holds undivided sway. From this standpoint, a game of Chess becomes a harmonious whole, the outlines of which I will endeavor to describe to you in this course of lectures.

The requisites in Chess are a board of sixty-four squares, and two bodies of men. We have, therefore, one great advantage over the general who is to lead an army into the field—we know where to find the enemy, and the strength at his disposal.

**9**

We have the gratifying knowledge that as far as material strength is concerned we shall be equal to our opponents. Nevertheless, our first step will be exactly analogous to that of a commander of an army. First of all we shall mobilize our troops, make them ready for action, try to seize the important lines and points which are yet wholly unoccupied. This proceeding will take, as a rule, no more than six moves, as we shall see later on. If we should neglect to do so, our opponent would avail himself of the opportunity thus given him, would quickly assail some vital point, and ere we could rally, the battle would be finished.

Let me, in illustration of my assertions, go over some well known little games, in which mistakes and the punishment thereof are clearly traceable.

| WHITE. | BLACK. |
|---|---|
| 1. P—K4 | P—K4 |
| 2. Kt—KB3 | P—Q3 |
| 3. B—B4 | P—KR3 |

So far, with the exception of the last move, Black has played quite well. He has opened lines for his two Bishops and the Queen, and now should bring out his QKt to B3. Instead of that, afraid of some premature attack, he quite unnecessarily makes a move that does not give additional force to any of his pieces.

| 4. Kt—QB3 | B—Kt5 |
|---|---|

A mistake. The Knights should be first developed, then the Bishops.

| 5. | Kt×P | B×Q |
| 6. | B×Pch. | K—K2 |
| 7. | Kt—Q5 checkmate | |

Another tune to the same song.

| | WHITE. | BLACK. |
|---|---|---|
| 1. | P—K4 | P—K4 |
| 2. | Kt—KB3 | Kt—KB3 |
| 3. | Kt×P | Kt—QB3 |

Black evidently believes in the principle of quick development, and even neglects to take White's KP, in order to gain time.

| 4. | Kt×Kt | QP×Kt |
| 5. | P—Q3 | B—QB4 |
| 6. | B—Kt5 | |

A mistake; he ought to guard against the threatened Kt—Kt5 with B—K2. Now he is overtaken by a catastrophe.

| 6. | ...... | Kt×P |
| 7. | B×Q | B×Pch. |
| 8. | K—K2 | B—Kt5 checkmate |

Another variation.

| | WHITE. | BLACK. |
|---|---|---|
| 1. | P—K4 | P—K4 |
| 2. | P—KB4 | P×P |

White, in order to aid his development, sacrifices a Pawn. Whether with good reason or not, we shall not argue for the present.

| 3. | B—B4 | Q—R5ch. |
|---|---|---|
| 4. | K—B | P—Q4 |

An excellent move. Black also sacrifices a Pawn, to invest it, so to say, in facilities for bringing out his pieces.

| 5. | B×P | P—KKt4 |
|---|---|---|
| 6. | Kt—KB3 | Q—R4 |
| 7. | P—KR4 | |

A good move, which gives our Rook something to do. The attack on Black's Pawn, however, is only an apparent one for the moment, because both the Kt and KRP are pinned.

| 7. | ...... | P—KR3 |
|---|---|---|

He ought to develop a piece, for instance, B—Kt2. This omission will cost him the game.

| 8. | B×Pch. | Q×B |
|---|---|---|

Not K×B, on account of (9) Kt—K5ch.

| 9. | Kt—K5 | Q—Kt2 |
|---|---|---|
| 10. | Q—R5ch. | K—K2 |
| 11. | Kt—Kt6ch. | K—Q |
| 12. | Kt×R | Q×Kt |
| 13. | P×P | |

And now we have two Pawns and an excellently placed Rook for two pieces, while Black's pieces are all still at home, and his King in an unsafe position. Between fairly even players the issue of the game is therefore decided in favor of White.

Let me go over the moves which frequently occur in games of a close character.

| WHITE. | BLACK. |
|--------|--------|
| 1. P—K4 | P—K3 |
| 2. P—Q4 | P—Q4 |
| 3. Kt—QB3 | Kt—KB3 |
| 4. B—KKt5 | B—K2 |

He ought to first exchange the Pawns, and then bring his Bishop to K2. In such manner he would obtain an almost unassailable position.

| 5. B×Kt | B×B |
|---------|------|
| 6. Kt—KB3 | Castles |

There is no necessity for him to castle so early. His first aim should be to bring his Q side into action. For instance: (6) .... P×P; (7) Kt×P, Kt—Q2; (8) B—Q3, P—QKt3; (9) Castles, B—Kt2, would be, although not the very best, a sufficiently safe plan for bringing his pieces out.

| 7. B—Q3 | P—QKt3 |
|---------|--------|
| 8. P—K5 | B—K2 |
| 9. P—KR4 | |

White consistently takes aim against Black's K side. Black's Q side pieces have so little bearing upon the actual scene of battle that his game is already greatly compromised.

| 9. ...... | B—Kt2 |
|-----------|--------|

The only comparatively safe move would have been B—QR3.

BLACK.

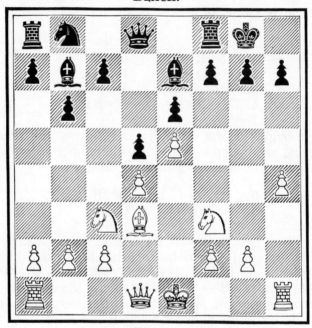

WHITE.

| 10. | B×Pch. | K×B |
|-----|--------|-----|
| 11. | Kt—Kt5ch. | K—Kt3 |

If instead K—Kt sq.; (12) Q—R5, B×Kt; (13) P×B, P—B3; (14) P—Kt6, and mate cannot be avoided.

| 12. | Kt—K2 | B×Kt |
|-----|-------|------|
| 13. | P×B | P—KB4 |

If Q×P; (14) Kt—B4ch., K—B4; (15) Q—Q3ch., K—Kt5; (16) Q—R3ch., K×Kt; (17) Q—B3 mate.

| 14. | KtP×P *e.p.* | K—B2 |
| 15. | Kt—B4 | R—Rsq. |

To protect himself against White playing R—
KR7. But his defence is of no avail, as his cruel
foe does not allow him a moment's repose.

| 16. | Q—Kt4! | R×Rch. |
| 17. | K—Q2 | P×P |

What shall he do? If R—R2; (18) Q×KPch.,
K—B; (19) Kt—Kt6 mate.

| 18. | Q—Kt6ch. | K—K2 |
| 19. | Q—Kt7ch. | K—K |
| 20. | Q—Kt8ch. | K—K2 |
| 21. | Q×Pch. | K—B |

First White drives the Black K into the most dangerous spot, and then comes the finishing stroke—

| 22. | R×R | K—Kt2 |
| 23. | R—R7ch. | K×R |
| 24. | Q—B7ch. | K—R |
| 25. | Kt—Kt6 checkmate. | |

If we again critically glance over the few variations that we have gone through, we must be
struck by one fact, namely, that the losing side
had the greater part of his army in positions where
they had no bearing whatever upon the questions
at issue. They might have been just as well any-
where else but on the board. I have formulated
the rules for the development of the pieces according to my own experience over the board, and, I

think, also in accordance with established facts, in the following manner:—

I. Do not move any Pawns in the opening of a game but the K and the Q Pawns.

II. Do not move any piece twice in the opening, but put it at once upon the right square.

(In my practice I have usually found it strongest to post the Kts at B3, where they have a magnificent sway, and the KB somewhere on his original diagonal, if not exposed to exchange, at QB4.)

III. Bring your Kts out before developing the Bishops, especially the QB.

IV. Do not pin the adverse KKt (by B— KKt5) before your opponent has castled.

In regard to Rule I you will sometimes, especially in Q side openings, find it a better plan to advance the QBP two squares before obstructing it by your QKt. This, however, is the only exception, where the violation of the principles just laid down, is unquestionably justified. You will see that, according to this plan, the mobilization takes altogether six moves, consumed in the development of two Pawns, the two Knights, and the two Bishops. You may be obliged to spend some of your time in the beginning of a game for the exchange of a pawn or a piece, or it may be necessary to make one or two defensive moves. But the real business of development ought to be accomplished in no more than six separate moves devoted to that purpose.

## No. 2

Gentlemen: We have given in our former Lecture the theory of the first part of a game of Chess, and have, to a certain extent, attempted to prove and to illustrate it. It now remains to put it to practical test. For this purpose we shall discuss to-day a popular form of opening called the Ruy Lopez, from the name of the Spanish bishop who invented it. It consists in the following three moves:—

| WHITE. | BLACK. |
|--------|--------|
| 1. P—K4 | P—K4 |
| 2. Kt—KB3 | Kt—QB3 |
| 3. B—QKt5 | |

Of course you will at once perceive that the threat, which White's last move seems to imply, viz., B×Kt, followed by Kt×P, is only an apparent one, as Black will regain his Pawn easily. We are, therefore, at liberty to make any developing move we please. According to the principles of our last Lecture either (3) .... P—Q3, or (3) .... Kt—KB3 should be done. Both of these moves very frequently *are* made, and, on the whole, with satisfactory results. Personally I favor the immediate development of the Kt, as P—Q3 deprives the KB of the possibility to occupy the file from QB4.

**3.** ......          **Kt—KB3**

White's next move may be (4) Kt—QB3, or P—
Q3, which would give him a solid and, on the
whole, strong game.  But these variations would
not present any special difficulty to Black, who
could continue, for instance, with P—Q3 and after-
ward adopt exactly the tactics recommended in
our first Lecture.  White has, however, other
continuations at his disposal which give him a
harassing attack, which Black must exercise great
judgment to meet.

**4.  Castles**

What is Black to do next?  According to our
principles he may play either B—K2, or B—B4,
and actually either of these moves may be made
without any real danger.  But this is not the
question at issue.  The Black KKt attacks the
White KP, which White has left unguarded.  Is
Black to accept the offer?  I consider this matter
at some length, because it frequently presents
itself, for instance, in all gambits.

My answer is this: When you are conscious not
to have violated the rules laid down, you should
accept the sacrifice of an important Pawn, as the
KP, QP, or one of the BPs.  If you do not, as a
rule, the Pawn which you have rejected will become very troublesome to you.  Do not accept the
sacrifice, however, with the idea of maintaining
your material advantage at the expense of development.  Such a policy never pays in the end.  By
far the better plan is to give the Pawn up after
your opponent has made some exertions to gain it.

By the same process, through which your opponent has achieved greater scope for his pieces, you will then always be able to recoup yourself, and, as a rule, be a gainer in the bargain.

I am speaking rather authoritatively in this matter, as I cannot prove my assertions for the moment. However, I do not ask you to believe me blindly. In the course of this Lecture, and in those that are to follow, enough, I trust, will be found to warrant what I said. This principle is the one amendment which I wish to add to the four rules given in the last Lecture.

4.  . . . . . .            Kt×P

This move exposes Black to some danger, and I do not think it would be right of me to show you only how Black gets out of it with flying colors. We shall come to a fuller understanding of the possibilities of the position when we, in some variations, let Black pay the penalty for his daring.

5.  R—Ksq

Not the best move, but one that most naturally suggests itself.

5.  . . . . . .            Kt—Q3

To gain time by the attack on the White Bishop.

6.  Kt—QB3        Kt×B
7.  Kt×P

Cunning play. If Black now takes one of the Knights he loses, _e. g._,

| A | 7. | ...... | KKt×Kt |
|---|----|--------|--------|
|   | 8. | Kt×Ktch. | B—K2 |
|   | 9. | Kt×B! | Kt×Q |
|   | 10. | Kt—Kt6ch. | Q—K2 |
|   | 11. | Kt×Q and remains a piece ahead | |

| B | 7. | ...... | QKt×Kt |
|---|----|--------|--------|
|   | 8. | R×Ktch. | B—K2 |
|   | 9. | Kt—Q5! | Castles |
|   | 10. | Kt×Bch. | K—Rsq |

Now see White's mode of attack, which is rather instructive and of frequent occurrence.

> 11.  Q—R5          P—KKt3

White threatened mate in two by Q×Pch., etc

> 12.  Q—R6          P—Q3

White mates in two.   Which is the move?

> 13.  R—R5          P×R
> 14.  Q—B6 checkmate

Let us now return to the original position, at Black's seventh turn to move.

> 7.  ......          B—K2

We thus intercept the dangerous file against our King and develop a piece—two great advantages.

| 8. | Kt—Q5 | Castles |
|----|-------|---------|
| 9. | Kt×Kt | QP×Kt |
| 10. | Kt×Bch. | K—R |
| 11. | Kt×B | Q×Kt |
| 12. | P—Q3 | Q—B4 |
| 13. | B—K3 | P—KR3 |

And Black's game is, if anything, preferable. You
see how quickly White's attack has spent itself out.
But then he did not make the best of his position
at move 5. Let us therefore return to that point.

5. P—Q4

We develop and attack at the same time, while
our Pawn cannot be taken, viz.: (5) .... P×P;
(6) R—K, (6) P—KB4; (7) Kt×P, threatening
P—KB3, and should win.

5. ...... B—K2

Kt—Q3 instead leads to an early exchange of
Queens. The resulting position is rather somewhat
in favor of White, viz.: (5) .... Kt—Q3; (6)
B×Kt, QP×B; (7) P×P, Kt—B4; (8) Q×Qch.,
K×Q; (9) R—Qch., K—K; (10) Kt—QB3,
B—K2; (11) P—KR3, B—K3; (12) B—KKt5
with an occasional onslaught of the K side Pawns.

6. Q—K2

The last move is more aggressive than P×P at
once, which would allow Black time to do anything
he pleases, for instance, to castle at once, or to advance P—Q4. Consider the following variation as
an example of what is likely to follow after: (6)
P×P, P—Q4; (7) P×P e.p., Kt×P; (8) B×
Ktch., P×B; (9) Kt—K5, B—Kt2, and in spite
of his doubled Pawn Black's pieces are excellently
placed.

6. ...... Kt—Q3
7. B×Kt KtP×B

not QP×B, which would open the Q file to White's Rook, *e. g.*, (7) ...., QP×B; (8) P×P, Kt—B4; (9) R—Q, B—Q2.

The Black QB and Q are now so badly placed that White has an opportunity of bringing the game to a virtual finish by energetic attack. (10) P—K6, P×P; (11) Kt—K5, threatening both the Bishop and Q—R5ch., and should therefore win.

8.   P×P        Kt—Kt2

BLACK.

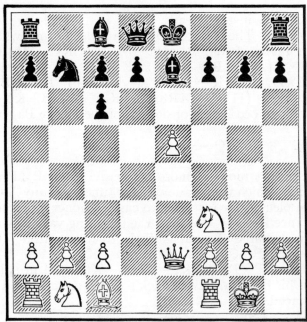

WHITE.

We have now come to a critical stage. Black's pieces have retired into safety, ready, with one single move, to occupy points of importance. White, on the contrary, has the field to himself, but he can do nothing for the present, as there is no tangible object of attack. Various attempts have been made to show that White has here the superior position. I do not believe that White has any advantage, and am rather inclined to attribute the greater vitality to the party that has kept its forces a little back.

Ere we proceed any further let us consider some sub-variations: (9) Kt—Q4, Castles; (10) R—Q, Q—K; (11) R—K (to prevent either P—B3 or P—Q4), Kt—B4 (not to be recommended, although in frequent use); (12) Kt—QB3, B—R3; (13) Q—Kt4, Kt—K3; (14) Kt—-B5, K—R; (15) Kt—K4; and Black is quite helpless against the threat R—K3 and R3, etc. Or again: (9) Kt—Q4. Castles; (10) R—Q, Q—K; (11) R—K, Kt—B4; (12) KtB3, Kt—K3; (13) Kt—B5, P—Q4; (14) P×P *e. p.*, P×P; (15) Q—Kt4, P—Kt3; (16) B—R6, Kt—Kt2; (17) Kt×Bch., Q×Kt; (18) Q—Q4, and wins at least the exchange.

These variations show that it must be Black's aim to post his KB on a line where he can do some effectual work, and to advance his QP. From this position the following variations suggest themselves:—

|     |         |         |
| --- | ------- | ------- |
| 9.  | Kt—Q4   | Castles |
| 10. | R—Q     | Q—K     |
| 11. | R—K     | B—B4!   |
| 12. | Kt—Kt3  | B—Kt3   |
| 13. | Kt—B3   | P—Q4    |

and, if Black has not the best of the position, at least all danger is past. Another attempt:

| | | |
|---|---|---|
| 9. | Kt—B3 | Castles |
| 10. | Kt—Q4 | B—B4 |
| 11. | B—K3 | Q—K |
| 12. | P—KB4 | P—Q3 |

Black's pieces are again all well in play. White has, to a certain extent, compromised himself by the advance of the KBP.

We can now announce our final judgment. The defence considered, initiated by (3) ...., Kt—KB3, yields, in all respects, a satisfactory game to the second player.

## No. 3

Gentlemen: Though we have established in our last Lecture a line of play which will yield a good defence to the usual form of the Ruy Lopez, we may nevertheless look at others well worth noticing. Truth derives its strength not so much from itself as from the brilliant contrast it makes with what is only apparently true. This applies especially to Chess, where it is often found that the profoundest moves do not much startle the imagination.

A defence which is frequently played is initiated in the third move by advancing the QRP against our Bishop. I need not dwell on the point that this move is against the principles of our first Lecture, just as much as Kt—KB3 is in accordance with them. Neither does it, I believe, lead to an even game—an opinion which I shall attempt to substantiate in the following variations:—

| | | |
|---|---|---|
| 1. | P—K4 | P—K4 |
| 2. | Kt—KB3 | Kt—QB3 |
| 3. | B—QKt5 | P—QR3 |

White has now the option to exchange his Bishop against the adverse Kt, or to retreat it. As a general rule, it is not good policy to exchange in the early stages of a game the long reaching Bishop against the Knight, whose power does not extend beyond a certain circle. Therefore

| | | |
|---|---|---|
| 4. | B—QR4 | Kt—KB3 |

(4) .... P—Q3 is not to be recommended, on account of (5) P—Q4, B—Q2; (6) P—B3, P—B4; (7) KP×P, P—K5; (8) Kt—Kt5, with an all-round healthy position for White.

| | |
|---|---|
| 5. | Castles |

Both, (5) Kt—B3 or P—Q3, would yield White a good game. His chances of success are, however, greatly increased if he adopts a more dashing form of attack.

5. ...... Kt×P

Black cannot well refuse the acceptance of the (momentary) sacrifice, as otherwise White will obtain a good position by P—Q4, followed by P—K5; or else (5) .... P—Q3; (6) P—Q4, P—QKt4; (7) P×P, with a good game.

6. P—Q4          P—QKt4
7. B—Kt3        P—Q4

Black would be rather venturesome to take the QP, because White could continue with R—K and molest the Black KKt, in fact, finally win it.

8. P×P          B—K3
9. P—QB3

White's last move is an exception to the rule we have hitherto followed, to develop as quickly as possible. The game has assumed already a character of its own, which in consequence adds to the importance of some pieces in preference to others. Our KB is destined to serve as the backbone of our attack against the Black King, in the moment (which must soon arrive) that he castles on the K side. We therefore preserve it against the possible attack of the Black Kts, which are driven into exposed points.

9. ...... KB—B4

K2 would also be a favorable spot for the Bishop, but it seems necessary to reserve this point for the QKt.

Moreover, there is a certain want of protection on the Q side, for which you provide by putting the Bishop into the rear of your Pawns.

No fault is now to be found with Black's *development*, all his pieces being well in play; but his Pawn position on the Q side is compromised. How White will take advantage of that weakness the following will explain:—

| 10. | Kt—Q2 | Castles |
| 11. | B—B2 | |

BLACK.

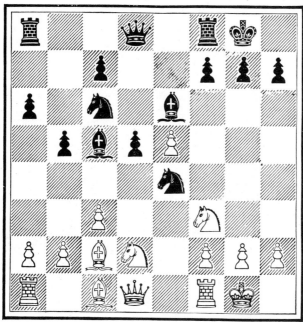

WHITE.

The position becomes now very instructive. Whether the twice attacked Kt is removed, or exchanged, or guarded, in each case White obtains a splendid game.

| A 11. | ...... | Kt—Kt4 |
|---|---|---|
| 12. | Kt×Kt | Q×Kt |
| 13. | Kt—K4 | Q—K2 |
| 14. | Kt×B | Q×Kt |
| 15. | B—K3 | Q—K2 |
| 16. | P—KB4 | |

sooner or later threatening P—B5, with a beautiful position.

| B 11. | ...... | Kt×Kt |
|---|---|---|

What is the right move now—the move which adds most to the power of our pieces?

| 12. | Q×Kt! |
|---|---|

Now we threaten Kt—Kt5. With P—KR3 he cannot defend, as Q—Q3 would force P—KKt3, and thus the gratuitous win of the RP. If B—K2, R—K, to be followed by Kt—Q4, and then speedily P—KB4, would give us the pull; so he plays

| 12. | ...... | Kt—K2 |
|---|---|---|
| 13. | P—QKt4 | B—Kt3 |
| 14. | Kt—Kt5 | |

BLACK.

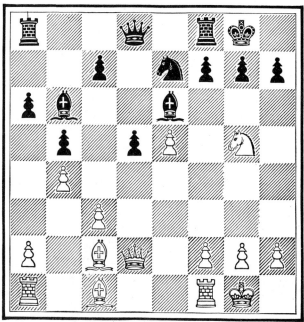

WHITE.

Let us consider some variations in this interesting position:

|   |     |        |         |
|---|-----|--------|---------|
| A | 14. | . . . . . . | P—KR3 |
|   | 15. | Kt—R7  | R—K     |
|   | 16. | Kt—B6ch. | P×Kt  |
|   | 17. | Q×P    | P—B4    |
|   | 18. | B—Kt5  |         |

and Black is without defence.

| B | 14. | ...... | Kt—Kt3 |
|---|-----|--------|---------|
| | 15. | B×Kt | RP×B |
| | 16. | Q—B4 | |

threatening Q—R4, etc.

| | 16. | ...... | R—K |
|---|-----|--------|------|
| | 17. | Q—R4 | P—KB3 |
| | 18. | Q—R7ch. | K—B |
| | 19. | Q—R8ch. | B—Kt |
| | 20. | P×P | P×P |
| | 21. | Kt—R7ch. | K—B2 |
| | 22. | B—R6 and wins. | |

| C | 14. | ...... | B—KB4 |
|---|-----|--------|--------|
| | 15. | B×B | Kt×B |
| | 16. | Q—Q3 | P—KKt3 |
| | 17. | Q—R3 | P—R3 |
| | 18. | P—KKt4 | P×Kt |
| | 19. | P×Kt | Q—K2 |
| | 20. | R—K | |

Now we threaten the advance of our KB Pawn, to be followed up by Q—R6. So Black can do nothing else but

| | 20. | ...... | P—KB3 |
|---|-----|--------|--------|
| | 21. | P×KtP | P×P |
| | 22. | R×P | |

regardless of expense,

| | 22. | ...... | B×Pch. |
|---|-----|--------|---------|
| | 23. | K—R | Q—Kt2 |
| | 24. | Q—K6ch. | K—R |
| | 25. | R×KtP winning easily. | |

What must strike us most forcibly in this variation, is the tremendous power of our K side

Pawns, which have swept everything before them, as a matter of fact, totally annihilated the opposing force, while at the same time Black's Q side Pawns have been lazy spectators of the fight.

Let us go back again to where we left off the examination of our principal line of play.

| 11. | ...... | P—KB4 |
| 12. | P×P *e. p.* | |

Also Kt—Kt3 and then QKt—Q4 would be a good continuation.

| 12. | ...... | Kt×P |
| 13. | Kt—Kt5 | B—KKt5 |
| 14. | QKt—B3 | Kt—K4 |
| 15. | B—B4 | Kt×Kt |
| 16. | P×Kt | B—B |

B—Q2 would be still worse on account of the rejoinder (17) B—K5.

| 17. | Q—Q3 | P—KKt3 |

He has no other mode of defence. If, for instance, (17) ...., Kt—K5; (18) Kt×Kt, P×Kt; (19) Q×Q, etc.

| 18. | Kt×P | B—B4 |

Obviously, if (18) ...., K×Kt; (19) Q×Pch., K—R; (20) K—R would speedily decide the issue

| 19. | Kt×Ktch. | R×Kt |
| 20. | Q—Q2 | B×B |
| 21. | B—Kt5 (or else Q×B). | |

with a winning advantage.

My object, in thus diving down into the depths of this position, is not by any means to provide your memory with ballast. All I want to show is that the superior position will perforce become overpowering, whichever turn you may try to give to the game. And why have we got what we termed the superior position? You see, Black's Q side Pawns do not *work*, they only require protection, while White's Pawns, either actively or only as potentials of future action, are contributing to White's success.

But we must not yet rest satisfied with the analysis. There may yet be a way of escape, at move 11, namely,

| 11. | ...... | B—B4 |
| 12. | Kt—Kt3 | B—QKt3 |
| 13. | P—QR4 | |

The unfortunate Q side Pawns serve us again as a mark for attack. Now we threaten to exchange the Pawns, then the Rook, and to gain the QP.

| 13. | ...... | R—QKt |

This move seems to be the only practicable reply, as otherwise, for instance, after Kt—K2, QKt—Q4 would become very dangerous.

| 14. | KKt—Q4 | Kt×Kt |
| 15. | Kt×Kt | B×Kt |

or if (15) ...., B—Q2; (16) P×P, P×P; (17) Q—Q3.

| 16. | P×B | |

Now we have obtained our purpose. Firstly, we have two Bishops beautifully bearing down against the adverse K side; then Black's QBP is now kept backward by our Q Pawn, and will never be able to advance.

|     |     |       |
| --- | --- | ----- |
| 16. | ..... | B—Kt3 |

or else P—B3 will win a piece.

| 17. | P×P   | P×P    |
| --- | ----- | ------ |
| 18. | R—R7  | P—QB3  |
| 19. | P—B3  | Kt—Kt4 |
| 20. | R—R6  | R—B    |
| 21. | B—K3  | Kt—K3  |
| 22. | P—B4  | B×B    |
| 23. | Q×B   | Q—Q2   |

A desperate attempt to free himself by (23)....,
P—QB4 would fail against (24) P×P, P—Q5;
(25) R—Q6, R×P; (26) Q—Q3.

| 24. | P—B5   | Kt—Q |
| --- | ------ | ---- |
| 25. | Q—KB2  |      |

We now want our most powerful piece on the K side.

| 25. | ..... | K—R   |
| --- | ----- | ----- |
| 26. | Q—R4  | Q—Kt2 |

He must, after all, try to get something out of his Q side.

| 27. | P—B6  | P—Kt3  |
| --- | ----- | ------ |
| 28. | Q—R6  | Kt—K3  |
| 29. | R—R3  | R—KKt  |
| 30. | B—Q2  | Kt—B   |
| 31. | B—Kt4 |        |

and Black is quite helpless.

Again I beg to draw your attention to the difference of power exerted by the White and the Black Pawns. Taken all round you will perhaps agree with me when I declare that Black, by choosing the defence (3) ...., P—QR3 to the Ruy Lopez, unnecessarily damages his Q side Pawns, while the development of his pieces gives him no compensation for that disadvantage.

To relieve your chess nerves from the tension which they must have undergone to-day, allow me to introduce, as a finale, a more pleasing matter. In my match with Mr. Steinitz, that master chose, for a long while, a somewhat close defence to the Ruy Lopez, beginning with (3) P—Q3. The game usually ran as follows:—

| | | |
|---|---|---|
| 1. | P—K4 | P—K4 |
| 2. | Kt—KB3 | Kt—QB3 |
| 3. | B—Kt5 | P—Q3 |
| 4. | P—Q4 | B—Q2 |
| 5. | Kt—B3 | KKt—K2 |
| 6. | B—QB4 | |

threatening, of course, Kt—KKt5.

| | | |
|---|---|---|
| 6. | ...... | P×P |
| 7. | Kt×P | |

Now it seems that Black, in order to keep White's Queen at bay, has a good way of developing his KB by means of P—KKt3 and BKt2, where the Bishop certainly would have an excellent diagonal. This little plan, however, was never executed by

Mr. Steinitz, the reason appearing in what follows. If

    7. ......           P—KKt3
    8. B—KKt5

In order to take possession of the diagonal which
Black attempts to occupy.

    8. ......           B—Kt2
    9. Kt—Q5

attack and counter-attack.

    9. ......           B×Kt

Anything else would be clearly disadvantageous.
Black, of course, is now under the expectation
that White will continue with (10) Kt×Kt, when
B×P would allow Black to get out of danger. But
White has a more efficient move at his disposal:

    10. Q×B!

This is very awkward for Black. If now (10)
...., Kt×Q; (11) Kt—B6ch., K—B; (12)
B—R6 checkmate. So nothing remains but to
castle.

    10. ......           Castles
    11. Kt—B6ch.      K—R
    12. Kt—Kt4ch.    Kt×Q
    13. B—B6ch.       K—Kt
    14. Kt—R6 checkmate.

## No. 4

Gentlemen: The Evan's gambit, which in accordance with your desire I have chosen to-night as subject of discussion, is constituted by these four moves:—

| | | |
|---|---|---|
| 1. | P—K4 | P—K4 |
| 2. | Kt—KB3 | Kt—QB3 |
| 3. | B—B4 | B—B4 |
| 4. | P—QKt4 | |

There is no necessity for Black to accept the offer of the Pawn. On the contrary, if he retires with his Bishop to Kt3 in reply, he will, as White's last move has in no way furthered his development, gain a small but distinct advantage in position. The play which would then ensue will be of the following character:—

| | | |
|---|---|---|
| 4. | ...... | B—Kt3 |
| 5. | P—QR4 | P—QR3 |
| 6. | P—QB3 | Kt—KB3 |
| 7. | P—Q3 | P—Q3 |
| 8. | Castles | Kt—K2 |

soon to be followed by P—QB3 and PQ4. Black's pieces are all well placed, no matter whether White castles at his eighth turn to move, or defers that yet for some time. If White therefore sacrifices a Pawn by giving the gambit, Black sacrifices the sure prospect of positional advantage by taking it.

The idea of the gambit is very obvious. We want to continue, if B×P (or Kt×P), with

| | |
|---|---|
| 5. | P—QB3 |

and later on proceed with the advance of the QP, so as to obtain a very strong centre and to open several lines for the attack of the pieces. The Bishop can retire to either B4, R4, K2, to his own square, or to Q3, where he is not as badly placed as at first sight appears. The best players favor B—R4 or B4, with a preference for the former. If we retire to B4 the Bishop may be attacked again by P—Q4, while, on the contrary, B—R4 counteracts that advance. On the other hand, the Bishop at R4 will take away from the QKt an important point, from where he might attack the White KB. But taken all around,

     5.  ......            B—R4

seems to be the preferable move.

White has now two formidable continuations.

     6.  P—Q4

naturally suggests itself first, although it is not of such lasting effect as another move which we shall consider later on.

Black will answer

     6.  ......            P×P
     7.  Castles        P×P

The weakest point in Black's camp is the KBP, so we follow up our attack by

     8.  Q—Kt3

Black can reply with either Q—K2 or Q—B3. From K2 the Q has hardly any move that is not commanded by White's pieces, therefore

     8.  ......            Q—B3
     9.  P—K5

in the expectation of embarrassing Black's development, as neither the QP nor the KBP can advance for the present without being taken, with the effect that all lines are opened up to our pieces.

| 9. | ...... | Q—Kt3 |
| 10. | Kt×P | KKt—K2 |

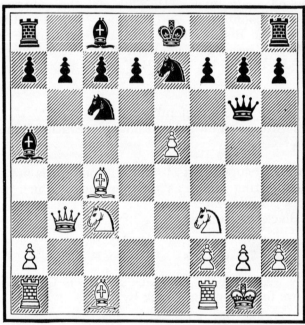

In this position we already see that White's attacking moves are pretty well exhausted. He has only a very unsatisfactory continuation.

11. B—R3

which gives to the Bishop a long file merely in exchange for another one.

This position has been subject of analysis for many decades, and several variations have been found which seem to leave Black with a comparatively safe K position and a Pawn ahead. None of the continuations given seem to be superior to the one that follows.

|     |        |        |
|-----|--------|--------|
| 11. | ...... | B×Kt   |

(This move was suggested by Mr. Lord during the lecture.)

|     |        |         |
|-----|--------|---------|
| 12. | Q×B    | P—QKt3  |
| 13. | B—Q3   | Q—R3    |

Not Q—R4, as (14) B×Kt, K×B; (15) P—K6, might follow.

|     |        |         |
|-----|--------|---------|
| 14. | KR—Q   | B—Kt2   |

and it is difficult to see in which way White will make good his minus of two Pawns.

This line of play, the so-called compromised defence of the Evans gambit, leads sometimes to very brilliant combinations. Let me give you an instance of this at move 11 of our principal variation.

|     |            |          |
|-----|------------|----------|
| 11. | ......     | Castles  |
| 12. | QR—Q       | KR—K     |
| 13. | Kt—K4      | Q×Kt     |
| 14. | B×Pch.     | K—B      |
| 15. | B—Kt8      | P—Q4     |
| 16. | P×P e. p.  | Kt×B     |
| 17. | Kt—Kt5     | Q—B4     |
| 18. | Q—B7ch.    | Q×Q      |
| 19. | Kt×P mate  |          |

Instead of (6) P—Q4, the greatest connoisseur of the Evans, Mr. Tschigorin, favors (6) castles, with the object of maintaining his centre. It cannot be doubted that this line of play is more in keeping with the original idea of the gambit.

Black, in accordance with the principles laid down in Lecture 1, must either play his QP or his KKt. It is usually the best policy when you are subject to a violent attack to move the QP, and when you are the aggressive party to develop your pieces first.

In the position before us

6. ...... P—Q3

appears therefore to be the allowed sounder play.

7. P—Q4       P×P
8. P×P        B—Kt3

leads to the "normal position" of the Evans. The five Pawns that White has gathered on his K wing against Black's four, exert a considerable amount of pressure on Black's pieces, the more so as Black will be obliged to leave his K on the dangerous side. It is true that Black may establish three Pawns to one on the other wing; but then it will take him a great deal of time to force the fighting on that side, while White's pieces will soon be in direction and ready for assault.

Various continuations have recently been recommended as best for White; but it seems to me that the old way of playing is as good as any. The line of play usually followed by the old masters is

| 9.  | P—Q5   | Kt—R4   |
| --- | ------ | ------- |
| 10. | B—Kt2  | Kt—K2   |
| 11. | B—Q3   | P—KB3   |
| 12. | Kt—B3  | Castles |

BLACK.

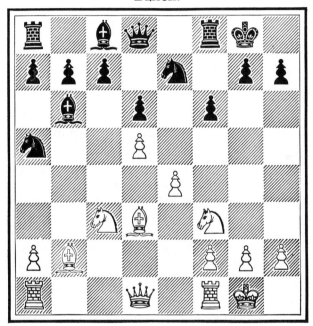

WHITE.

It is not my intention to analyze the position by the method usually followed, of simply enumerating all possible variations. Such analysis, unless it is very thorough, I contend, is quite useless. It certainly, as the experience of many centuries indisputably shows, would by no means exclude the possibility of committing grave errors, and it usually puts into obscurity the points of view from which the essential characteristics of the position may be deduced.

Without going into details, this much is certain, either

(*a*) Black will advance his KBP to B4; or,

(*b*) He will initiate an attack on the Q side with P—QB4, P—QR3, B—B2, P—QKt4, etc.; or,

(*c*) He will be content to break up White's strong centre by P—QB3.

There is, indeed, no other *plan de campagne* to follow.

As regards the first point, it is easily seen that such an advance would not increase the defensive strength of Black's position. It would open the file of the White QB, the point K4 to the White Kts (after the exchange of the Pawns), and probably facilitate the joint attack of the White KBP and KKtP.

(*b*) This was the plan of defence, or rather counter-attack, in Anderssen's tierce. White will obtain the advantage in the following manner:

| | | |
|---|---|---|
| 13. | K—R | Kt—Kt3 |
| 14. | Kt—Q2 | P—QB4 |
| 15. | P—KB4 | P—QR3 |
| 16. | Kt—K2 | B—B2 |
| 17. | Kt—B3 | P—QKt4 |
| 18. | P—B5 | Kt—K4 |
| 19. | Kt—B4 | |

This will represent pretty accurately the state of affairs ten or twelve moves after the normal position has been arrived at. It takes at least seven moves to bring the Black Pawns to their destination. In the meantime White is free to advance his KKt Pawn in two steps to Kt5, and to open up a pernicious attack against Black's K side.

(c) White's policy will be exactly as in (b), to advance his KBP. If Black exchanges the QBP against the QP, the KP will retake, and the Black QKt will be unfavorably situated. Black has in this variation practically no chance of winning, in spite of his extra Pawn, while the attack of White is very lasting and dangerous.

It seems then that the normal position will yield to White much better chances of winning than it will to Black.

If you want to simplify matters, I advise you to play

7.  ......          B—Kt3

at once, with the object of converting your extra material into positional advantage. If then (8) P×P, P×P; (9) Q×Q, Kt×Q; (10) Kt×P, Kt—KB3. Black's solid Pawns and good, sound development will make it hard to White to keep up the equilibrium, as his QRP and, more so, the QBP require constant care. If, on the other hand, (8) P×P, P×P; (9) Q—Kt3, Q—B3; (10)

B—Q5, KKt—K2; (11) B—Kt5, Q—Kt3; (12) QB×Kt, K×Kt; (13) B×Kt, Q×B; (14) Kt×P, Q—K3; (15) Q—R3, P—QB4 or K—B3, with two Bishops, a healthy development of forces and a solid position.

One of the finest games on record was played at a time when the analysis of the Evans gambit was not yet far advanced. It has been named "the evergreen partie." The leader of the White forces was Professor Anderssen.

|     |         |         |
| --- | ------- | ------- |
| 1.  | P—K4    | P—K4    |
| 2.  | Kt—KB3  | Kt—QB3  |
| 3.  | B—B4    | B—B4    |
| 4.  | P—QKt4  | B×P     |
| 5.  | P—B3    | B—R4    |
| 6.  | P—Q4    | P×P     |
| 7.  | Castles | P—Q6    |

A now obsolete defence.

|     |          |         |
| --- | -------- | ------- |
| 8.  | Q—Kt3    | Q—B3    |
| 9.  | P—K5     | Q—Kt3   |
| 10. | B—R3     | KKt—K2  |
| 11. | R—K      | P—QKt4  |
| 12. | B×P      | R—QKt   |
| 13. | Q—R4     | B—Kt3   |
| 14. | QKt—Q2   | B—Kt2   |
| 15. | Kt—K4    | Q—B4    |
| 16. | B×P      | Q—R4    |
| 17. | Kt—B6ch. | P×Kt    |
| 18. | P×P      | **R—Kt** |

BLACK.

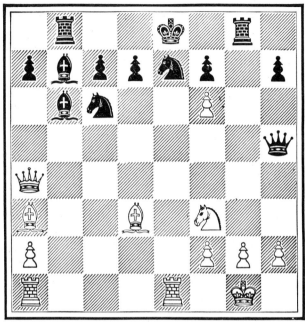

WHITE.

     19.   QR—Q

One of the most subtle and profound moves on record.

| 19. | ...... | Q×Kt |
| --- | --- | --- |
| 20. | R×Ktch. | Kt×R |
| 21. | Q×Pch. | |

Grand!

| 21. | ...... | K×Q |
| --- | --- | --- |
| 22. | B—B5doublech. | K—B3 |
| 23. | B—Q7checkmate | |

If at move 20 Black continues with (20) ...., K—Q; (21) R×Pch., K—B; (22) R—Q8ch., Kt×R; (23) Q—Q7ch. and mates in two more moves.

Gentlemen: According to the request you made to me last Monday, we shall consider to-day the King's Bishop's gambit, which, as you all know, is constituted by these moves:—

| | | |
|---|---|---|
| 1. | P—K4 | P—K4 |
| 2. | P—KB4 | P×P |
| 3. | B—B4 | |

If I remind you of Rule III you will admit that the development of the B is not in accordance with our fundamental principles. Actually the move of the KKt to B3 would be far stronger, as it leads to a fairly even game, while the KB gambit should be lost to the first player.

The defence will, before all, disturb the quiet course of White's development, by (3) ...., Q—R5ch., to which White is bound to answer with

4. K—B

According to the principles of development, either the QP or one of the Kts should move. White is threatening to bring forth an enormous force in no more than three moves, to bear upon the centre of the board, namely, Kt—KB3, Kt—QB3, P—Q4. Black dare not quietly submit to that, as for the moment his Q is exposed to danger. To keep the White K in his unsound position, to spoil the plan of White, and to aid the quick development of Black's forces, the best policy is the most aggressive one, that is, the one initiated by the sacrifice of the QP.

| 4. | . . . . . . | P—Q4 |
| 5. | B×P | |

Now, before anything else is undertaken

| 5. | . . . . . . | P—KKt4 ! |

Our Bishops have two long lines; our Kts have only one move to make to occupy points of importance, and to add to the firmness of our position. We can, therefore, spare the time for this advance of the KKtP, destined to protect our KBP against all possible attack, and to render the K side unsafe for White's pieces.

| 6. | Kt—KB3 | Q—R4 |
| 7. | P—KR4 | B—Kt2 |

An excellent reply. The Bishop not only protects the Rook, but guards the two centre points, Q4 (Q5), K5 (K4).

| 8. | P—Q4 | P—KR3 |
| 9. | K—Kt | Q—Kt3 |
| 10. | Kt—QB3 | Kt—K2 |

So far, everything went all right, because White consistently played for the development of his minor pieces. Now it becomes apparent that the White QR is awkwardly placed, and the QB no less. The K position need not give any anxiety, but the Q has somehow no good prospects of serving her cause. At the same time, Black is quite safe—there is only one weak point in his camp, the KBP—and any possible attacks of the White minor pieces in the centre are obviated by the clever sacrifice of the fourth move.

BLACK.

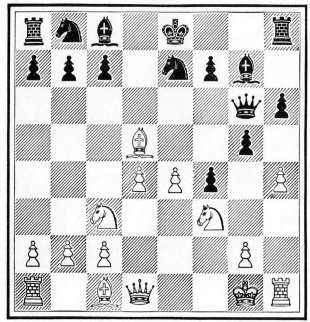

WHITE.

11.   Q—Q3

preparatory to B—Q2

11.   . . . . . .        P—QB3
12.   B—Kt3          B—Kt5!

Here the QB has a splendid position safe of all

possible attack by inferior pieces and with R4 as a safe retreat.

| | | |
|---|---|---|
| 13. | B—Q2 | Kt—Q2 |
| 14. | K—B2 | Castles Q side |

All the weakness of the White game becomes now at once apparent. His K and QP are exposed to the most direct attack of the hostile R and Kts, and KB. Try what he may, the day is gone. Black threatens B×Kt and Kt—K4. If (15) Kt—K2, Kt—QB4 wins directly. If (15) P×P, P×P; (16) R×R, B×R the danger is not obviated. If finally (15) Q—B4, B×Kt; (16) P×B, Kt—K4; (17) P×Kt, R×Bch.; (18) K—K, KR—Q; (19) Q×P, Q×Q; (20) B×Q, B×P; (21) B—Kt3, B×Kt; (22) P×B, Kt—Kt3, followed by Kt—K4, is at least *one* way of obtaining a great advantage.

Let us return to move 11, and vary White's play.

| | | |
|---|---|---|
| 11. | P—K5 | P—QB3 |
| 12. | B—K4 | B—KB4 |
| 13. | Q—K2 | Kt—Q2 |
| 14. | B×B | Kt×B |

White is obliged to undertake some kind of attack, or Black will Castle Q side, and the breakdown of White's centre will be practically certain.

| | | |
|---|---|---|
| 15. | Kt—K4 | P—KKt5 |

Now, at last, this advance is justified, because the
QP has lost its protection by the Q

| 16. | Kt—Q6ch. | K—B |
| 17. | Kt×Kt | P×Kt |

and wins a piece or (17) P—R5, P×Kt or (17)
Kt—K, Q×Kt; (18) P×Kt, B×Pch., and should
win.

We must therefore come to the conclusion that
the KB gambit is unsound.  I will not pretend
that there is any right and wrong in Chess from
an ethical standpoint, but by what right should
White, in an absolutely even position, such as
after move 1, when both sides have advanced
P—K4, sacrifice a Pawn, whose recapture is quite
uncertain, and open up his K side to attack?  And
then follow up this policy by leaving the check of
the Black Queen open?  None whatever!  The
idea of the gambit, if it has any justification, can
only be to allure Black into the too violent and
hasty pursuit of his attack.  If, therefore, we can
obtain by sound and consistent play the superiority of position, common sense triumphs over
trickery, and rightly so.

When the analytical and theoretical knowledge
of Chess was not so far advanced as at the present
time, famous players frequently chose the lively
forms of development which are the outcome of
gambits.  One of these games, though unsound
in the highest degree, has been of such excep-

tionally brilliant character that it was honored by the players of the time with a special name. We know it as "The Immortal Partie." Here its moves follow:

| | WHITE. Anderssen. | BLACK. Kieseritzky. |
|---|---|---|
| 1. | P—K4 | P—K4 |
| 2. | P—KB4 | P×P |
| 3. | B—B4 | Q—R5ch. |
| 4. | K—B | P—QKt4 |
| 5. | B×P | Kt—KB3 |
| 6. | Kt—KB3 | Q—R3 |
| 7. | P—Q3 | Kt—R4 |
| 8. | Kt—R4 | P—QB3 |
| 9. | Kt—B5 | Q—Kt4 |
| 10. | P—KKt4 | Kt—B3 |
| 11. | R—KKt | P×B |
| 12. | P—KR4 | Q—Kt3 |
| 13. | P—R5 | Q—Kt4 |
| 14. | Q—B3 | Kt—Kt |
| 15. | B×P | Q—B3 |
| 16. | Kt—B3 | B—B4 |
| 17. | Kt—Q5 | |

I have not dwelt on the constant violation of principle by Black. The consequence of his imaginative schemes is that none of his pieces are developed; and here White could have smashed Black up by advancing first P—Q4.

| 17. | ...... | Q×P |
| 18. | B—Q6 | |

BLACK.

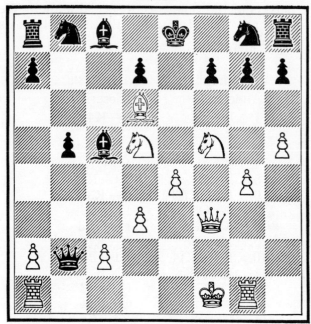

WHITE.

A fine coup.

| 18. | ...... | Q×Rch. |
|---|---|---|
| 19. | K—K2 | B×R |
| 20. | P—K5 | |

Obstructing the line from QR8 to KKt2.    A glorious finish.

| 20. | ...... | Kt—QR3 |
|---|---|---|
| 21. | Kt×Pch. | K—Q |
| 22. | Q—B6ch. | Kt×Q |
| 23. | B—K7 checkmate | |

Gentlemen: As you have expressed the desire to have one of the close openings discussed, I have chosen to-night as subject of discussion the popular and important French defence, which arises when Black replies to White's P—K4 with P—K3.

1.   P—K4            P—K3

This defence had for a long time the reputation of leading to a dull kind of game.   In later years it has been found that it gives opportunities for a great many violent attacks of a character which it is difficult to obtain in any other opening.

The difference between Black's first move P—K3 and the other P—K4, commonly chosen, is twofold.   The Pawn at K3 blocks the long diagonal of the Black QB reaching up to KR6, which is, I might say, almost naturally open to him.   On the other hand, in the ordinary games which open with P—K4 on each side, the White KB can take up a very strong diagonal from QB4 pointing toward the initially weakest point in Black's camp, the square KB2. This line also is obstructed. These two peculiarities give to the French defence a character of its own, which, with good play on the part of White, it should never lose.

The move, which gives to the White pieces as much freedom as can be obtained in one single move, is

2.   P—Q4

And just so on the part of Black.

2.   ......            P—Q4

As early as this, opinions greatly differ as to the

best continuation to be chosen by White. The attack has, namely, the choice—

    *a.* To sacrifice the KP.
    *b.* To exchange it.
    *c.* To advance it.
    *d.* To guard it.

(*a*) May be at once dismissed. If we play (3) Kt—KB3, P×P; (4) Kt—Kt5, this may lead to a tricky game, but with sound and energetic play on the part of Black, a great advantage ought to accrue to the second player. (*c*) is equally inadvisable, as the early advance of Pawns unbacked by pieces always is. This may be the line of play to follow:—

| | | |
|---|---|---|
| | 3. P—K5 | P—QB4 |
| | 4. P—QB3 | Kt—QB3 |
| | 5. Kt—KB3 | Q—Kt3 |
| | 6. B—K2 | KKt—K2 |
| | 7. Castles | Kt—B4 |
| or | 5. P—KB4 | Q—Kt3 |
| | 6. Kt—KB3 | B—Q2 |
| | 7. P—QKt3 | Kt—R3 |
| | 8. B—K3 | Kt—B4 |
| | 9. B—B2 | P×P |
| and if | 10. P×P | B—Kt5ch. |

You see White comes, without compensation, into great difficulties.

(*b*) The exchange of the Pawns in the third move

      3. P×P         P×P

leads to a very even game, in which the advantage of the first move counts for very little. The game might go on

|  |     | White | Black |
|---|-----|-------|-------|
|   | 4.  | Kt—KB3 | Kt—KB3 |
|   | 5.  | B—Q3 | B—Q3 |
|   | 6.  | Castles | Castles |
|   | 7.  | B—KKt5 | B—K3 |
|   | 8.  | QKt—Q2 | QKt—Q2 |
|   | 9.  | R—K | R—K |
|   | 10. | Kt—K5 | Kt—B |
| or | 10. | P—B3 | Kt—B |
|   | 11. | Q—B2 | P—B3 |
|   | 12. | R—K2 | Q—B2 |
|   | 13. | B×Kt | P×B |
|   | 14. | QR—K | Kt—Kt3 |
|   | 15. | P—KKt3 |  |

When the advantage of the doubled Rooks on the open file is counterbalanced by the strong position of the two Black Bishops, and Black may even have, on account of the somewhat questionable exchange at move 13, the superior game.

A game well worth knowing is the one played by Blackburne against Schwarz in Berlin, 1881. (1) P—K4, P—K3; (2) P—Q4, P—Q4; (3) P×P, P×P; (4) Kt—KB3, B—Q3; (5) B—Q3, Kt—KB3; (6) Castles, castles; (7) B—KKt5, B—KKt5; (8) Kt—B3, Kt—B3; (9) B×Kt, Q×B. White is greedy to win a Pawn, and voluntarily exchanges B v. pinned Kt—always a great mistake. (10) Kt×P, Q—R3; (11) P—KR3, Kt×P, and Black (Blackburne) won easily, as White's K position is exposed.

The want of *finesse* in variation (b) is accounted for by the Pawn position. The Pawn at Q4 takes away a good square from the KKt; it blocks the file of the B from K3 to R7, or from QB3 to

KKt7; it further obstructs the Q file. If the two Pawns on the Q file could by some means be exchanged, the position would assume a very different character. As it is, they are never to be got rid of, unless with the friendly assistance of your opponent.

(d) The strongest move that comes under this heading is (3) Kt—QB3. A custom has lately sprung up of posting this Kt at Q2, where it obstructs the QB and the Q. A good reply against such sickly policy is always to open up all lines quickly; for instance, in the given case to advance P—QB4. To the move actually chosen Black's answer is, as a rule,

3. ...... Kt—KB3

Now most players choose as continuation

4. B—KKt5

A move unquestionably against the rules of development, to which Black ought to reply by

| 4. | ...... | P×P |
| 5. | Kt×P | B—K2 |
| 6. | B×Kt | P×B |
| 7. | Kt—KB3 | P—KB4 |
| 8. | Kt—Kt3 | P—QB4 |

And Black will have a very good game.

The better play is the more audacious one,

| 4. | P—K5 | KKt—Q2 |
| 5. | P—KB4 | |

According to one of Mr. Steinitz's principles, which is, whenever you advance your Pawn to K5, back it up by P—KB4 as soon as possible.

| 5. | . . . . . . | P—QB4 |
| 6. | P×P | |

This exchange of Pawns is imperative. In former years White invariably tried, in close games, to keep his P at Q4 by backing it up by P—QB3. This policy has the two great disadvantages that it leaves a weak Pawn at Q4 open to attack, and that it opens a file (the QB file) for the intervention of the Black Rooks.

BLACK.

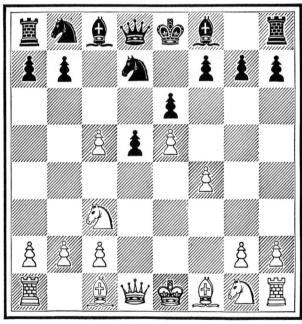

WHITE.

| 6. | . . . . . . | B×P |
| 7. | Q—Kt4 | Castles |
| 8. | B—Q3 | Kt—QB3 |
| 9. | Kt—B3 | |

White now threatens the sacrifice which is so common in close games, that of B against RP.

| 9. | . . . . . . | P—KB4 |
| 10. | Q—R3 | Kt—Kt5 |
| 11. | P—KKt4 | |

White has only *one* aim—to make play on the K side, while the development of the Black QB is yet unaccomplished. He therefore does not lose any time by advancing the QRP, and has now a fine attacking game. Assume, for instance,

| 11. | . . . . . . | Kt×Bch. |
| 12. | P×Kt | Kt—Kt3 |
| 13. | P—Q4 | B—Kt5 |
| 14. | R—KKt | Q—B2 |
| 15. | B—Q2 | Kt—B5 |
| 16. | P—R3 | Kt×B |
| 17. | K×Kt | |

And the White game is altogether preferable—or

| 11. | . . . . . . | Kt—Kt3 |
| 12. | P—QR3 | Kt×Bch. |
| 13. | P×Kt | B—Q2 |
| 14. | P—QKt4 | B—K2 |
| 15. | Kt—Q4 | |

To make another attempt

|     |            |            |
| --- | ---------- | ---------- |
| 11. | . . . . . . | Q—Kt3      |
| 12. | P×P        | Kt×Bch.    |
| 13. | P×Kt       | R×P        |
| 14. | Kt×P       |            |

and should win.

If, then, Black is reduced at move 9 to the necessity

|    |            |         |
| -- | ---------- | ------- |
| 9. | . . . . . . | P—KR3   |

White can, nevertheless, pursue the policy of aggression by immediately advancing his KKtP.

|     |        |
| --- | ------ |
| 10. | P—KKt4 |

To take advantage of the opportunity thus offered of opening up the adverse K side.

Black may strengthen his defence at move 6

|    |            |         |
| -- | ---------- | ------- |
| 6. | . . . . . . | Kt—QB3  |
| 7. | P—QR3      | B×P     |

The Pawn must be taken now, as otherwise P—QKt4 will save it. To capture it with Kt does not appear to be superior, as the Kt is not very happily placed at B4, and obstructs the KB somewhat.

|    |       |         |
| -- | ----- | ------- |
| 8. | Q—Kt4 | Castles |

Here Black may defend himself by P—KKt3, when a very difficult game will ensue, in which, however, the Black K side Pawns will furnish White with good objects of attack.

|    |      |        |
| -- | ---- | ------ |
| 9. | B—Q3 | P—QR3  |

It is difficult to suggest a different line of play. Black must do something to bring the White Q side under a certain pressure, as otherwise White would gratuitously obtain a good K side attack. The advance of the QRP and the QKtP seem to be the only means of accomplishing that purpose.

10.  Kt—KB3

threatening B×Pch.

| | | |
|---|---|---|
| 10. | ...... | P—KB4 |
| 11. | Q—R3 | P—QKt4 |
| 12. | P—KKt4 | P—KKt3 |
| 13. | Q—Kt3 | |

A very important manœuvre, but it is difficult to say whether this move or Q—Kt2 will, in the end, prove superior.

| | | |
|---|---|---|
| 13. | ...... | K—R |

Again, it is hard to find out better play, as White threatens to obtain a passed K Pawn by P×P.

14.  P—KR4

with a first rate attack.

I think you will agree with the proposition that I have to lay down, viz., that (3) Kt—KB3 subjects the defence to a difficult game.   As a good reply to (3) Kt—QB3 I advise you to choose the following continuation

| | | |
|---|---|---|
| 3. | ...... | P×P |
| 4. | Kt×P | Kt—KB3 |
| 5. | Kt—Kt3 | P—QB4 |
| 6. | Kt—B3 | Kt—B3 |
| 7. | B—K3 | Q—Kt3 |

| or, | 5. | B—Q3 | P—QB4 |
|---|---|---|---|
|  | 6. | P×P | B×P |
|  | 7. | Kt×B | Q—R4ch. |
|  | 8. | P—B3 | Q×Kt |
|  | 9. | B—K3 | Q—B2 |
|  | 10. | Kt—B3 | Kt—B3 |
|  | 11. | Castles | P—QKt3 |

It is dangerous to Castle into the two B files; so Black first brings out his B—Kt2, R to Q square, and waits with moving his King until White has spent some of his accumulated "potential force" (gathered in the centre). You may vary your tactics at move 5 by playing: (5) ...., Kt—B3; (6) P—QB3, P—K4 with a good game.

One word about close games in general. The rules of quick development, as laid down in Lecture 1, require *one* amendment, viz., do not obstruct your QBP by your QKt (unless you wish to open the game at once by P—K4), and advance that Pawn as early as you can to QB4.

After the Easter holidays we shall discuss the general principles of the remaining parts of the game, when much that has been said hitherto will obtain a different and a deeper meaning.

## Nos. 7 and 8

Gentlemen: So far we have considered the first part of a game of Chess, called the opening, and usually embracing about a dozen moves. The object of development is, as we have seen, to get the pieces into action, and to place them on favorable lines, in order to have them at hand when you intend to make them "work." The process of making pieces in Chess do something useful (whatever it may be) has received a special name: it is called the attack. *The attack is that process by means of which you remove obstructions.* That is so in every fight, whether it be a battle, or a fight with swords, or a boxing encounter, this definition will always apply.

Let us compare the game of Chess to some other fight—for instance, to a battle. Two armies opposite each other are attempting to destroy, or at least to frighten, each other. The armies, if about even in numbers, and also as far as favorable position is concerned, will each have a superiority in some quarter which will enable them not only to hold their opponents there in check, but also to drive them out of their position. Three things determine whether an attack should be made, and, if so, in which manner. First of all, the proportion of the attacking force to that directly opposing it in numbers; secondly, the nature of the surroundings; thirdly, the relation of the forces engaged to the rest of the army.

The third consideration will influence the *time* in which the attack must be executed, whether rapidly (if the advent of reserve force must under all circumstances be avoided) or step by step; in other words, it determines whether we should make it our object to economize in time, or in material force at our disposal.

The surroundings will, in part, add to the defensive strength of our opponents, and in part take away from it. Their character will determine which part of the hostile force is exposed to the effect of our weapons, and which is shielded; where we can advance with comparative safety, and which part of the ground we have to traverse rapidly; in other terms, which are weaknesses to be assailed, and which our strong points toward which to advance. The first consideration will tell us whether, after we have gained, by the methodical destruction of the obstacles in our way, a position of advantage, we are able to destroy or drive away the opposing force; or whether the object of our attack, if obtained, is a sufficient compensation for the lives sacrificed. If, in any kind of fight, the rules for attack are laid down, the three things mentioned must be studied.

In Chess the soldiers are the men and the general is the mind of the player. If anything that is subject to the possibility of an attack be a weak point, all men, and especially the King and the heavy pieces (Queen and Rooks), would be such; we shall, however, call a weakness only such pieces, or group of pieces, as in proportion to their importance have a defect in defensive strength, for instance: a Queen, that has only a very limited range of action, or a Pawn that cannot advance nor yet be protected by other Pawns. A weak point is a *square*—not necessarily occupied —which can only be attacked by heavy pieces like the Queen or the Rooks, so that Pawns, Knights and Bishops, or eventually also Rooks, protected by other men, are there quite safe. Our opponent's weak points we shall name strong points, speaking from our point of view. If we can occupy a strong point by one of our pieces, which has from there a large sphere of action, the battle is often half decided in our favor.

Obstructions in Chess are pieces of minor importance which intercept the lines of action of our men. It is, as a rule, easier to remove them when they are hostile men, because we may threaten them by so many of our own pieces that we can finally safely capture them; it is different when, for instance, one of our own Pawns, blocked by one of the Pawns or pieces of the enemy, stands in our way; and worse still when this Pawn is isolated; the only way of removing it by force consists then usually in placing a piece under the protection of this Pawn, and forcing the exchange of that piece.

Let us now consider the initial position. The

ultimate object of every attack in Chess is given beforehand—it is the capture by force of the hostile King. For that purpose we must command nine squares, the eight around the King and the one he occupies; we can reduce that number only by driving the King to the edge of the board, or by forcing his own pieces to obstruct his escape. Finally, the checkgiving piece must not be liable to capture, nor must any of the hostile pieces be able to intercept its line of attack. This is the "work to be done," and it is enormous, considering the large amount of force gifted with capacity to capture and obstruct at the enemy's disposal. This task is still made more difficult by the other one which you have to perform—to protect your own King against your opponent's assaults.

The Chess world went about the task thus voluntarily undertaken, and attempted to solve the problem involved by the humanly most direct method; it simply tried it, piling variation on variation, correcting and re-correcting them, for, say, two thousand years. Many beautiful games were played, and startling discoveries made, but the real problem was never solved. And why, may we ask, have for so long a time the exertions of the best brains of the human race continually failed? There is one answer whose cogency is irresistible, an answer whose truth seems to be proved by experience beyond doubt, viz., there *is* no solution, and for this reason the resources on each side are so evenly balanced that the trifling advantage of the first move is not sufficient to force the defence to resignation.

This admitted, we must begin, before entering upon our task, with the supposition that the initial position has been differentiated to such an extent that the win of the game becomes possible to the one or other party. After having granted this much the problem is transformed, and it assumes the following shape: the balance of position and forces has at least been partly disturbed, and to checkmate the King of the inferior force becomes a feasible achievement.

Whether a nearly balanced position allows a forced win to the one or the other party depends usually on the slightest differences, so much so, indeed, that it would be a hopeless undertaking to search for certain rules, or a mathematical formula that would give you its solution without the application of intellectual power in each special case. The question involved is of such a complicated nature that the only way to obtain an answer is to divide the board into parts, to analyze the partial questions by the experimental method, and to finally draw the sum total of all the answers.

Now, given a position in Chess where, on the one wing (for instance, the K side), we have the superiority, on another (the Q side or the centre) we may be at a disadvantage, but where, on the whole, our advantage is prevailing, in what manner are we to make capital out of that superiority? The answer depends, of course, on the analysis of the position; but if this analysis is methodical it will greatly acquire clearness and sharpness, and the mental labor required will be reduced to a minimum.

The moves in Chess are of three kinds, they are either

(*a*) Developing, *i. e.*, bringing new force into play.

(*b*) Attacking, *i. e.*, making pieces threaten the hostile men, give a check, threaten a checkmate, etc.; in other words, making pieces *do* something, or *work*.

(*c*) Serving defensive purposes, *i. e.*, giving protection to a weak point, obstructing an important line, etc.; in other words, *undoing* the work of the hostile men.

What kind of move is required is determined by the exigencies of the position. If you have a large superiority of force in a quarter where the enemy has important weaknesses, like the King or the Queen in a bad position, etc., you must assail quickly. Every one of your moves must be intended to do much. Your reserve force must be made useful for the attack with as much gain of time as possible—by attacking, for instance, some weaknesses while on the way—and the reserve forces of the opponent must be kept back, if possible, by obstructions that you can place in their way (think of Morphy's Pawn sacrifices for that purpose). The devices are manifold, but the variations, on account of the many forced moves on the part of the defence, are usually few, and therefore subject to direct analysis. Of such attacks we say that their "pace" is quick.

All the games given (especially the French defence of the previous lecture) have contained attacks of quick pace. Here follows another.

BLACK.

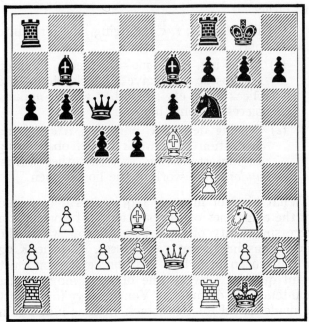

WHITE.

The game (International Tournament, Amsterdam) went on

| 1. | Kt—R5 | Kt×Kt |
| 2. | B×Pch. | K×B |
| 3. | Q×Ktch. | K—Kt |
| 4. | B×P | K×B |
| 5. | Q—Kt4ch. | K—R2 |
| 6. | R—B3 | P—K4 |
| 7. | R—R3ch. | Q—R3 |
| 8. | R×Qch. | K×R |
| 9. | Q—Q7 | B—KB3 |

| 10. | Q×B | K—Kt2 |
|-----|-----|-------|
| 11. | R—KB | QR—Kt |
| 12. | Q—Q7 | KR—Q |
| 13. | Q—Kt4ch. | K—B |
| 14. | P×P | B—Kt2 |
| 15. | P—K6 | R—Kt2 |
| 16. | Q—Kt6 | P—B3 |
| 17. | R×Pch. | B×R |
| 18. | Q×Bch. | K—K |
| 19. | Q—R8ch. | K—K2 |
| 20. | Q—Kt7ch. | |

and wins.

When your superiority is not clearly defined, you must be satisfied with attacking in a moderate pace, advancing on your strong points, and methodically creating new ones near your opponent's line of defence. Then the *plan* is everything, and the time a matter of secondary importance (compare the 3d, 4th, 5th and 6th game given in these lectures). Generally the "pace" of your attack must slacken down the less pronounced your advantage is. A very good player will seldom give you opportunities for violent and short attacks, which require an amount of acting force that is often underrated.

Some of Morphy's games:—

| 1. | P—K4 | P—K4 |
|----|------|------|
| 2. | P—KB4 | P×P |
| 3. | B—B4 | P—Q4 |
| 4. | P×P | B—Q3 |
| 5. | Kt—QB3 | Kt—KB3 |
| 6. | P—Q4 | Castles |
| 7. | KKt—K2 | P—B6 |

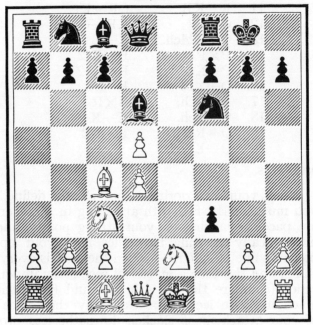

WHITE.

The White King stands in an obstructed file, so Morphy sacrifices his Pawn to prevent the King from castling with safety. It will be remarked that after the sacrifice the defensive power of the White KR and KB Pawn becomes very weak, both of these Pawns being isolated.

8. P×P       Kt—R4
9. P—KR4

It would have been better to defend by a developing move, such as (9) B—K3, when the following play might ensue: (9) ...., R—K; (10) Q—Q2, Q—K2; (11) Kt—K4, B—KB4; (12) B—Q3.

|     |          |     |
|-----|----------|-----|
| 9.  | ...... | R—K |
| 10. | Kt—K4    |     |

Occupying one of White's *strong points*, only to be attacked by the KBP or QB, therefore an excellent obstruction.

|     |          |          |
|-----|----------|----------|
| 10. | ......   | B—Kt6ch. |
| 11. | K—Q2     | B—Q3     |
| 12. | K—B3     |          |

Here he unnecessarily exposes himself to new dangers. P—B3 would have provided a safe retreat to the King.

|     |          |          |
|-----|----------|----------|
| 12. | ......   | P—QKt4   |

Quickly opening up all the lines on the side which the White King has chosen as refuge.

|     |          |          |
|-----|----------|----------|
| 13. | B×P      | P—QB3    |

Now he threatens Q—R4ch., so he indirectly forces White to remove the well-posted Kt from K4.

|     |          |          |
|-----|----------|----------|
| 14. | Kt×B     | Q×Kt     |
| 15. | B—R4     | B—R3     |
| 16. | R—K      | Kt—Q2    |
| 17. | P—Kt3    | Kt—Kt3   |
| 18. | B×P      | QR—B     |

Every one of Black's pieces has now long open files, in consequence of the energetic attacking manœuvres of the last six moves.

19.   K—Q2

Black threatened to win a piece by Kt or Q takes Pawn.   K—Kt2 would have lost immediately on account of (19) ...., B×Kt; (20) R×B, R×R; (21) Q×R, Kt—R5ch., either winning the Queen or checkmating the King in the next move.

| 19. | ...... | R×B |
|-----|--------|-----|
| 20. | P×R | B×Kt |
| 21. | R×B | Q×Pch. |
| 22. | K—K | Q—Kt8ch. |
| 23. | K—Q2 | R—Qch. |
| 24. | K—B3 | Q—B4ch. |
| 25. | K—Kt2 | Kt—R5ch. |

(26) resigns, for if P×Kt, Q—Kt5mate; if K—Kt, (26) Kt—B6ch., winning first the Queen and then the Rook.

His famous game against Paulsen in the New York Tournament runs as follows:

| WHITE. | BLACK. |
|--------|--------|
| Paulsen | Morphy |
| 1.   P—K4 | P—K4 |
| 2.   Kt—KB3 | Kt—QB3 |
| 3.   Kt—B3 | Kt—B3 |
| 4.   B—Kt5 | B—B4 |
| 5.   Castles | Castles |
| 6.   Kt×P | R—K |
| 7.   Kt×Kt | |

This capture only develops Black. It would have been quite as good to retire with the Kt to B3 and to follow this up, if (7) ...., Kt×P by (8) P—Q4.

| | | |
|---|---|---|
| 7. | ...... | QP×Kt |
| 8. | B—B4 | P—QKt4 |
| 9. | B—K2 | |

The Black Pawns by thus advancing do not, of course, gain in defensive strength, but Black is so far ahead in development that White will never be able to take advantage of that weakness.

| | | |
|---|---|---|
| 9. | ...... | Kt×P |
| 10. | Kt×Kt | R×Kt |
| 11. | B—B3 | |

If here (11) P—QB3, which looks at first sight stronger, then Black will assail the castled King, which for the present is the only support of the KR and KKt Pawn. The game might proceed (11) ...., Q—R5; (12) P—KKt3, Q—R6; (13) B—B3, R—R5; (14) P×R, B—Q3; or (12) P—Q4, B—Q3; (13) P—KKt3, Q—R6; (14) P—KB4, B—Q2; (15) B—B3, R—K2; when Black will double his Rooks on the K file and obtain a sound position with many attacking possibilities.

| | | |
|---|---|---|
| 11. | ...... | R—K3 |
| 12. | P—B3 | |

A somewhat elaborate process for so simple an object. First, P—Q3 was the proper play.

| | | |
|---|---|---|
| 12. | ...... | Q—Q6 |

This is one of the rare cases in which a heavy piece like the Queen can with success be used for the purpose of obstruction. The Queen cannot be attacked in her present situation by any hostile man, but exerts a considerable amount of pressure, preventing, for instance, such moves as Q—B2 or B—K2.

| | | |
|---|---|---|
| 13. | P—QKt4 | B—Kt3 |
| 14. | P—QR4 | P×P |
| 15. | Q×P | B—Q2 |
| 16. | R—R2 | |

This move may serve as a preparation for Q—B2. White evidently is beginning to feel the restraint which he suffers through the blockade of his QP by the adverse Queen. His plan, however, is frustrated by Black, whose attack has already become ripe for a decisive blow. If (16) Q—R6 instead, Black's best reply seems to be (16) ...., Q—B4; (17) P—Q4, QR—K; (18) B—K3, P—QB4; (19) KtP×P, B×P; (20) Q—R5?, R—KKt3, with a winning advantage, for if (21) K—R, Q×B, (22) P×Q, B—B3, leaves White helpless; therefore White's best would be (20) Q—K2, B—Kt3; (21) B—Kt4, R×B; (22) B×Q, R×Q; (23) B×B, with an even ending.

| | | |
|---|---|---|
| 16. | ...... | QR—K |

The strongest move for development and simultaneously for attack. Black threatens now Q×Rch.

| | |
|---|---|
| 17. | Q—R6 |

BLACK.

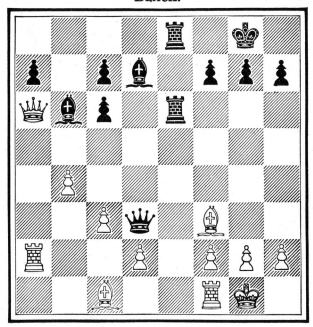

WHITE.

| 17. | ...... | Q×B |
|---|---|---|

An effective, surprising, and beautiful coup.

| 18. | P×Q | R—Kt3ch. |
| 19. | K—R | B—R6 |

Black threatens B—Kt7ch., followed by B×P mate. R—KKt is no safeguard, as after the exchange of the Rooks the QR will checkmate him. Nor would (20) Q—Q3 mend matters, as Black will answer with P—KB4, and if then (21) Q—B4ch., by K—B.

| 20. | R—Q | B—Kt7ch. |
| 21. | K—Kt | B×Pch. |
| 22. | K—B | B—Kt7ch. |

He might have decided the issue by R—Kt7, with the double threat R×Pch., tc., and R×RP.

| 23. | K—Kt | B—R6ch. |
| 24. | K—R | B×P |
| 25. | Q—B | |

His only resource.

| 25. | ...... | B×Q |
| 26. | R×B | R—K7 |

Again binding the hostile QP to his post.

| 27. | R—R | R—R3 |
| 28. | P—Q4 | |

At last!

| 28. | ...... | B—K6 |
| 29. | Resigns, for if (29) B×B, R (R3) ×Pch. (30) K—Kt, R—Kt7 checkmate. | |

Let us now pass over to more recent times.

| WHITE. | BLACK. |
| Anderssen. | Steinitz. |
| 1. P—K4 | P—K4 |
| 2. Kt—KB3 | Kt—QB3 |
| 3. B—Kt5 | Kt—B3 |
| 4. P—Q3 | P—Q3 |
| 5. B×Ktch. | |

This exchange is decidedly uncalled for. Black's QR gains thereby an open file, as well as the QB.

White has no compensation whatever; for to speak in the early stage of a game of the weakness of a double Pawn or an isolated Pawn for end game purposes is nothing but a chimera.

| | | |
|---|---|---|
| 5. | ...... | P×B |
| 6. | P—KR3 | P—Kt3 |

Black has already the advantage, and can therefore afford to lose a move for development, which will later on support his plan of attack.

| | | |
|---|---|---|
| 7. | Kt—B3 | B—KKt2 |
| 8. | Castles | Castles |
| 9. | B—Kt5 | P—KR3 |
| 10. | B—K3 | P—B4 |

An excellent coup. Black's plan, as will be seen, is to make the fighting on the K side with his Pawns; he therefore keeps the White QP back, to preserve the obstructions in the centre.

| | |
|---|---|
| 11. | R—Kt |

It would have been much more to the interest of White to forestall the imminent attack, for instance, by (11) Q—Q2, K—R2; (12) P—KKt4, Kt—Kt; (13) Kt—R2, P—B4; (14) P—B3.

| | | |
|---|---|---|
| 11. | ...... | Kt—K |
| 12. | P—QKt4 | P×P |
| 13. | R×P | P—QB4 |
| 14. | R—R4 | B—Q2 |
| 15. | R—R3 | P—B4 |

The White K Pawn, which intercepts the B file from QB3, blocks the KP and holds back the QP, dare not be removed. It is, therefore, an excellent object of attack.

| 16. | Q—Kt | K—R |
| 17. | Q—Kt7 | P—QR4 |
| 18. | R—Kt | P—R5 |
| 19. | Q—Q5 | Q—B |

White's game suffers for want of design. There is no possible object in all this manœuvring of the heavy pieces. His policy should have been one of defence, which he might conduct on the Kt—R2, P—KB3 *a. s. o.*, and perhaps successfully

| 20. | R—Kt6 | R—R2 |

In order to have his Queen free for the following threat, (21) ...., P—KB5; (22) B—Q2, B×P; (23) P×B, Q×P; (24) Kt—R2, P—B6, etc.

| 21. | K—R2 | P—KB5 |
| 22. | B—Q2 | P—Kt4 |
| 23. | Q—B4 | Q—Q |
| 24. | R—Kt | Kt—B3 |
| 25. | K—Kt | Kt—R2 |

The RP shall advance and then the KtP, to be followed by Kt—Kt4, where the Kt will have in conjunction with his advanced Pawns a commanding sway. Mark how carefully all this is prepared. No strong point is left to the White party in the rear of the Black Pawns, nor in front of them, during the whole of the tedious process.

| 26. | K—B | P—R4 |
| 27. | Kt—Kt | P—Kt5 |
| 28. | P×P | P×P |
| 29. | P—B3 | Q—R5 |
| 30. | Kt—Q | Kt—Kt4 |
| 31. | B—K | Q—R7 |

79

BLACK.

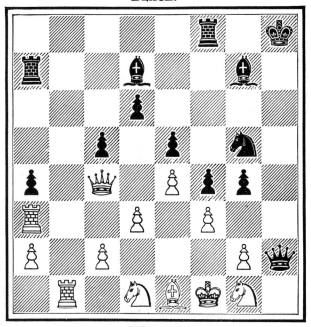

WHITE.

Here we have the beau ideal of the concluding
stages of a King side attack supported by a chain
of Pawns. If P×P, all the lines are opened by
P—B6 with tremendous effect. White cannot
much improve his position, as his pieces have no
space to execute any movements. So Black has
any amount of time to prepare the finishing stroke.

| 32. | P—Q4 | P×BP |
| 33. | KtP×P | Kt—R6 |
| 34. | B—B2 | Kt×Kt |
| 35. | P×BP | |

Of course, if (35) B×Kt, B—R6ch. wins.

| | | |
|---|---|---|
| 35. | ...... | Q—R6ch. |
| 36. | K—K | |

or (36) K×Kt, B—KB3 the White King being quite helpless.

| | | |
|---|---|---|
| 36. | ...... | Kt×Pch. |
| 37. | R×Kt | Q×R |

and Black won easily a few moves later.

Do not overlook how the apparently unimportant sixth move on the part of White was the real reason of all the trouble that he had to undergo later.

| WHITE. | BLACK. |
|---|---|
| Steinitz. | Zukertort. |
| 1. P—K4 | P—K4 |
| 2. Kt—KB3 | Kt—QB3 |
| 3. P—Q4 | P×P |
| 4. Kt×P | Kt—B3 |

According to our rules this should be the strongest reply. It certainly is a move that answers all purposes.

| | |
|---|---|
| 5. Kt—QB3 | B—Kt5 |
| 6. Kt×Kt | KtP×Kt |
| 7. B—Q3 | P—Q4 |
| 8. P×P | P×P |
| 9. Castles | Castles |
| 10. B—KKt5 | P—B3 |
| 11. Kt—K2 | B—Q3 |
| 12. Kt—Kt3 | |

The Kt occupies a square which White would do better to reserve for the Bishop. (12) Kt—Q4 seems therefore preferable.

| | | |
|---|---|---|
| 12. | ...... | P—KR3 |
| 13. | B—Q2 | |

BLACK.

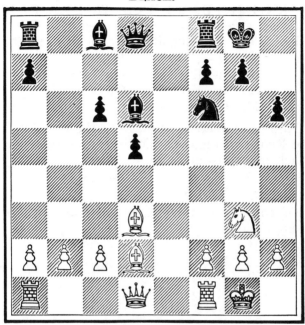

WHITE.

| 13. | ...... | Kt—Kt5 |

Excellent! Black now threatens Q—R5. If White replies by (14) P—KR3, then Kt×P; (14) K×Kt, Q—R5; (15) Q—B3, P—KB4 winning.

| 14. | B—K2 | Q—R5 |
| 15. | B×Kt | B×B |
| 16. | Q—B | B—K7 |

What he purposes with this is not very clear. He ought to strike hard while White is yet behind in the development of his Rooks, thus: (16)

...., P—KB4; (17) B—B4, B—B4; (18) R—K,
P—KKt4; (19) B—K3, B×B; (20) P×B, P—B5,
with an excellent attack; or even (16) B—Q2
will give him a lasting attack, difficult to meet.

| 17. | R—K | B—R3 |
| 18. | B—B3 | P—KB4 |
| 19. | R—K6 | QR—Q |
| 20. | Q—Q2 | |

Now he threatens Q—Q4, or the doubling of
the Rooks on the open file; but mark how finely
Black frustrates all this.

| 20. | ...... | P—Q5 |
| 21. | B—R5 | |

Of course he cannot take the Pawn without
losing a piece.

| 21. | ...... | R—Q2 |
| 22. | R×B | R×R |
| 23. | B—Kt4 | Q—B3 |
| 24. | R—Q | R—Q4 |
| 25. | B×R | Q×B |
| 26. | Kt—R5 | Q—K |
| 27. | Kt—B4 | R—K4 |

Black is first to take the open file—a great advantage, which White should not have yielded at
move 26.

| 28. | P—KR4 | P—B4 |
| 29. | P—R5 | |

This manœuvre with the RP, which shall make
the position of the Kt unassailable, is misplaced.
The RP exposes itself only to the attack of the
Bishop.

| 29. | ...... | R—K5 |
| 30. | P—QB3 | |

This unnecessary advance is the principal reason of the speedy conclusion that follows. Black's play from now to the end is admirably consistent and strong.

| | | |
|---|---|---|
| 30. | ...... | Q—Kt |
| 31. | P—KKt3 | Q—K4 |
| 32. | Kt—Kt6 | Q—Q3 |
| 33. | Kt—B4 | P—Q6 |
| 34. | P—Kt3 | |

If (34) Kt×P, B×Kt; (35) Q×B, R—K8ch., wins the Rook or Queen.

| | | |
|---|---|---|
| 34. | ...... | P—B5 |
| 35. | R—Kt | K—R2 |
| 36. | K—R2 | Q—QKt3 |

First rate; he now threatens R—K7.

| | | |
|---|---|---|
| 37. | K—Kt | B—Kt2 |
| 38. | R—Kt2 | Q—QB3 |
| 39. | P—B3 | Q—B4ch. |
| 40. | Q—B2 | R—K8ch. |
| 41. | K—R2 | |

or (41) K—Kt2, R—K6.

| | | |
|---|---|---|
| 41. | ...... | Q×Qch |
| 42. | R×Q | B×P |

Decisive. The QP must now win.

| | | |
|---|---|---|
| 43. | P—KKt4 | B—K7 |

and Black won a few moves later.

If we glance critically over the games given, we find two rules confirmed:

(i.) Don't attack unless you have some tangible superiority, either in the stronger working of your pieces, or in longer reach.

Corollary: If you do, the reaction will place

your army in a critical position, and the inevitable counter-attack will find you in disorder.

(ii.) Let it be the first object of your attack to create strong points as near your opponent's camp as possible, and occupy them with pieces which have from there a large field of action.

Corollary: Try to force your opponent's Pawns to advance on the side where you attack.

| WHITE. | BLACK. |
| Dr. Noa. | Dr. Tarrasch. |
| --- | --- |
| 1. P—K4 | P—K4 |
| 2. Kt—KB3 | Kt—QB3 |
| 3. B—Kt5 | Kt—B3 |
| 4. Castles | Kt×P |
| 5. R—K | Kt—Q3 |
| 6. B—R4 | B—K2 |
| 7. Kt×P | Kt×Kt |
| 8. R×Kt | Castles |

Now Black's development is excellent, and the Pawn position unassailable.

| 9. P—Q4 | Kt—B5 |
| 10. R—K | P—Q4 |
| 11. P—QB3 | |

White has no time for such a move. (11) B—Kt3, Kt—R4; (12) Kt—B3, Kt×B; (13) RP× B, B—Q3; (14) Q—B3, P—QB3; (15) B—B4, is a sounder line of play.

| 11. ...... | B—KB4 |

Immediately bearing down on the weak points of White, Q3, QB2.

| 12. | Kt—Q2 | Kt×Kt |
| 13. | B×Kt | B—Q3 |
| 14. | Q—R5 | B—Kt3 |
| 15. | Q—R3 | |

This manœuvre has not much point. (14) B—QB2 is more to the purpose.

| 15. | ...... | P—QB3 |

From here to the end Black's play is simply classical. Mark now how finely Black will combine the advantage resulting from the weak position of the White Queen, the slight weakness contained in the loose and ineffective positions of the White Bishops, his own strongly posted QB, and the lack of protection of the White QKtP for a highly logical and successful attack.

| 16. | R—K2 | Q—Kt3 |
| 17. | B—Kt3 | P—QR4 |

Capital! Developing the QR, dislodging the obstruction, and keeping the QKtP in its unsafe position.

| 18. | B—K3 | P—R5 |
| 19. | B—Q | KR—K |
| 20. | R—B | P—KB4 |

Grand! He forces White to advance either the KKtP or KBP. In the latter case K5 becomes a very strong point, in the former the Q is obstructed, and the P position weakened.

| 21. | P—KB4 | R—K2 |
| 22. | QR—B2 | QR—K |
| 23. | B—B | Q—Kt4 |

preventing Q—Q3, and again bearing down on the central weak points of the White game.

| 24. | Q—B3 | Q—B5 |
|-----|-------|-------|
| 25. | P—QR3 | R—K5 |
| 26. | P—KKt3 | P—B4 |

To get his reserve force, the KB, into play.

| 27. | R×R | BP×R |
|-----|-------|-------|
| 28. | Q—K3 | Q—Q6 |
| 29. | Q×Q | P×Q |
| 30. | R—B2 | P—Kt4 |
| 31. | B—Q2 | B—K2 |
| 32. | P—B5 | B—B2 |
| 33. | R—B | P×P |
| 34. | P×P | B—B3 |
| 35. | B—QB3 | R—K5 |
| 36. | B—B3 | B×Pch. |
| 37. | K—Kt2 | |

A mistake. (37) B×B, R×B; (38) R—Q is by far the preferable policy.

| 37. | . . . . . . | B×B |
|-----|-------------|-----|

Energetic and decisive, but not very difficult to foresee.

| 38. | B×R | P×B |
|-----|-------|-------|
| 39. | P×B | B—Kt6 |

and White resigns, for after (40) K—B2, P—Q7; (41) K—K2, B—B5ch. he will lose his Rook.

ONE OF MY MATCH GAMES OF 1892.

| | WHITE. | BLACK. |
|-----|--------|--------|
| | Lasker. | Blackburne. |
| 1. | P—Q4 | P—Q4 |
| 2. | Kt—KB3 | Kt—KB3 |
| 3. | P—B4 | P—K3 |
| 4. | Kt—B3 | QKt—Q2 |
| 5. | B—B4 | P—B3 |

On account of the last move which is more or less forced (not to allow QKt—Kt5) the development chosen by Black is not advisable.

|     |              |          |
| --- | ------------ | -------- |
| 6.  | P—K3         | Kt—R4    |
| 7.  | B—Kt5        | B—K2     |
| 8.  | B×B          | Q×B      |
| 9.  | B—Q3         | P—KKt3   |
| 10. | Q—K2         | Castles  |
| 11. | Castles K side | P—KB4  |

Attacks on the K side in this opening have usually little hope of success. An inspection of the position will show that the K side does not present weaknesses that could be assailed. The fight is, therefore, in the centre and on the Q side.

|     |        |          |
| --- | ------ | -------- |
| 12. | KR—Q   | QKt—B3   |
| 13. | QR—B   | B—Q2     |
| 14. | Kt—K5  | B—K      |
| 15. | Q—B2   |          |

Black has, with his 11th move, stopped the advance of the White KP. The White Q is therefore now available for the Q's wing.

|     |        |          |
| --- | ------ | -------- |
| 15. | . . . . . . | R—Q |
| 16. | P—QR3  | Kt—Q2    |
| 17. | Kt—B3  | Kt—Kt2   |
| 18. | R—K    |          |

White intends a Q side attack; and, therefore, makes first preparations to take advantage of any forward movement that Black might undertake on the K side, beginning with P—B5.

|     |        |          |
| --- | ------ | -------- |
| 18. | . . . . . . | Kt—B3 |
| 19. | P—QKt4 | Kt—K5    |
| 20. | Kt—K5  | Kt×Kt    |

| 21. | Q×Kt | Kt—R4 |
|-----|------|-------|
| 22. | P—QR4 | Kt—B3 |
| 23. | P—Kt5 | Kt—Q2 |
| 24. | Kt—B3 | P×BP |

White threatened now P—B5, followed by P—R5 and P—R6, to establish a dangerous passed Pawn at B5.

| 25. | Q×P | Kt—Kt3 |
|-----|-----|--------|
| 26. | Q—Kt3 | P×P |
| 27. | P×P | B—B2 |
| 28. | Kt—K5 | R—B |
| 29. | R—R | |

The object of White's attack was to keep the QRP back, which is now indefensible.

| 29. | ...... | R—R |
|-----|--------|-----|
| 30. | R—K2 | KR—B |
| 31. | KR—R2 | Q—B2 |
| 32. | P—Kt3 | Q—B6 |
| 33. | Q×Q | R×Q |
| 34. | R×P | R×R |
| 35. | R×R | R—B2 |

The attack has now succeeded. White has the advantage of a Pawn plus on the K side. What remains is to convert this into positional superiority—not an easy process, as still there are hardly any assailable points in the Black camp.

| 36. | K—B | B—K |
|-----|-----|-----|
| 37. | K—K2 | K—B |
| 38. | K—Q2 | K—K2 |
| 39. | R—R3 | K—Q3 |
| 40. | P—B3 | R—B |
| 41. | P—K4 | R—B2 |

| 42. | R—R | R—B |
| 43. | P—R4 | R—B2 |
| 44. | R—QKt | R—B |
| 45. | K—K3 | K—K2 |
| 46. | P—R5 | |

The decisive manœuvre. If the P is taken, the two isolated RPs will be a splendid object of attack, well worth the sacrifice.

| 46. | ...... | K—B3 |
| 47. | P×P | P×P |
| 48. | R—KR | K—Kt2 |

Here, after some manœuvres to complete the third hour (we played eighteen moves an hour), the game went on at move 55, the position being unchanged.

| 55. | P—Kt4 | P×KtP |
| 56. | P×P | R—QR |
| 57. | P—Kt5 | |

threatening Kt—Kt4—B6. And so on.

| 57. | ...... | R—R6 |
| 58. | K—Q2 | R—R7ch. |
| 59. | K—K3 | R—R6 |
| 60. | K—B4 | Kt—Q2 |
| 61. | B—B4 | Kt—B |
| 62. | R—QB | |

The finishing stroke. The Rook will now enter *via* B7 into the Black camp.

| 62. | ...... | R—R4 |
| 63. | B—Q3 | B×P |
| 64. | R—B5 | |

and White won easily.

## No. 9

Gentlemen: The principles of defence will be the subject of our lecture to-night.

If the attack is the process through which obstructions are brought out of the way, the defence is the art of strengthening them, of giving firmness to your position, and of averting the blow directed against you. When your position is not inferior to that of your opponent, and he nevertheless makes preparations to attack you, disregard them altogether, develop reserve forces, avoid his attack by the slightest defensive movement possible (like a first-rate boxer, who in the nick of time and with an almost imperceptible movement evades the blow), and institute a quick counter-action. When you, however, have been unfortunate enough to compromise yourself, to give your opponent an undeniable reason for and tangible object of attack (which may occur to the best and most cautious player as the result of an unsuccessful attack), you have to act very differently.

Also here common sense tells us exactly how to proceed. Every position will comprise points which are exposed to the action of the hostile forces and other points which are well guarded. An attack will direct itself in the first instance against your weakest points—for instance, against the KRP and KKtP after Castling, or against a Kt at B3, etc. You will, therefore, first of all, vacuate these points if they are occupied by men of great importance, the Queen or Rook, for instance, and also frequently a Knight and a Bishop; secondly, you will have to give them support; place the support in points which are not easily accessible by the enemy. The rest of your army is best employed in engaging the reserve force of the enemy —that is, such force which it will take him time and labor to utilize for the purposes of his attack.

The object of your opponent's attack is, generally speaking, to change the position of your men in a certain quarter by force. Abstain from changing it voluntarily, except for most forcible reasons. This is where most Chess players fail. In order, for instance, to avoid the approach of a Kt or Bishop to Kt5, they advance the RP to R3, losing a move, and besides, as a general rule, impairing the strength for purposes of defence of the chain of Pawns on the wing; or they advance the KKt Pawn to Kt3, to drive a Kt away posted at KB4, which, however well placed, is usually not half as dangerous as this move; or they retire a piece, because it may be driven away. Wait with all such moves until your antagonist has expended some time, material position, etc.—well, call it, taken altogether, some of the "power" at his disposal—on them.

For the rest your defensive movements must, of course, be subservient to the objects of the enemy's attack. You may, therefore, revert the rules for attack; let it be your object to prevent your opponent from creating strong points very near your line of defence. That comprises everything, as we shall see in the instances that are to follow.

| 1. | P—K4 | P—K4 |
| 2. | Kt—KB3 | Kt—QB3 |
| 3. | P—Q4 | P×P |
| 4. | Kt×P | Kt—KB3 |
| 5. | Kt×Kt | KtP×Kt |
| 6. | B—Q3 | P—Q4 |
| 7. | P—K5 | |

Black has followed up to this point the rules of development. He has given to White no object of attack, none of his pieces being in a weak position. White's attacking manœuvre is, therefore, premature.

| 7. | ...... | Kt—Kt5 |
| 8. | Castles | B—QB4 |
| 9. | P—KR3 | |

Now follows a clever stroke, which shows how unsound all White's play has been.

| 9. | ...... | Kt×KP |
| 10. | R—K | Q—B3 |
| 11. | Q—K2 | Castles |
| 12. | Q×Kt | Q×Pch. |
| 13. | K—R | B×RP |
| 14. | P×B | Q—B6ch. |
| 15. | K—R2 | B—Q3 |

and Black wins.

| 1. | P—K4 | P—K4 |
|---|---|---|
| 2. | Kt—KB3 | Kt—QB3 |
| 3. | P—Q4 | P×P |
| 4. | B—B4 | B—B4 |
| 5. | Castles | Kt—KB3 |

(5) . . . ., P—Q3 would be more in conformity with our rules. The next move is slightly inferior, and gives White the opportunity to a violent onslaught, which, however, in the face of Black's splendid development, fails against the best line of defence.

| 6. | P—K5 | P—Q4 |
|---|---|---|

The right reply. To remove the Kt would be vastly inferior. If, for instance, (6) . . . ., Kt—K5; (7) B—Q5 would disorganize Black's game; and if (6) . . . ., Kt—Kt5; (7) B×Pch., K×B; (8) Kt—Kt5ch., might follow.

| 7. | P×Kt | P×B |
|---|---|---|
| 8. | R—Kch. | B—K3 |
| 9. | Kt—Kt5 | Q—Q4 |

Not Q—Q2, as (10) Kt×B, P×Kt; (11) Q—R5ch., would allow White to gain the KB.

| 10. | Kt—QB3 | Q—B4 |
|---|---|---|
| 11. | P—KKt4 | Q—Kt3 |

Black must not take the KBP, as White would answer with (12) Kt—Q5, Q—Q; (13) R×Bch., P×R; (14) Kt×P. Now Black threatens to Castle Q side with a magnificent game, as White through his attacking manœuvres has vastly impaired the solidity of his position.

| 12. | QKt—K4 | B—Kt3 |
|-----|--------|-------|
| 13. | P—KB4 | Castles Q side |
| 14. | P—B5 | B×P |
| 15. | P×B | Q×P |

At last White has recouped himself in material, but at what an expense! He is three Pawns behind, his King is in a totally unsafe position, his enemy is brilliantly developed, and the QP and QBP, far advanced and well protected, are ready for decisive action whenever the slightest opportunity is offered. All this for a minor piece.

| 16. | P×P | KR—K |
|-----|------|------|
| 17. | Kt—Kt3 | P—Q6ch. |
| 18. | B—K3 | B×Bch. |
| 19. | R×B | Q—B4 |

or Q×Kt winning. Similar conclusions follow in any variations that White may choose after move 13. Therefore let us go back to that position, and vary the attack.

        13.   Kt×BP

A bold sacrifice, to maintain the attack. If K or Q takes Kt, Kt—Kt5 will regain the piece, with an excellent position. If B×Kt, White must be satisfied with driving the King into a somewhat exposed position by (14) P×P, Q×P; (15) Kt—B6ch., K—Q; (16) Q—B3, with good attacking possibilities against the exposed King. Black, however, has just as bold a reply, which utterly turns the tables and gives him the attack against the weakened K side of White.

95

BLACK.

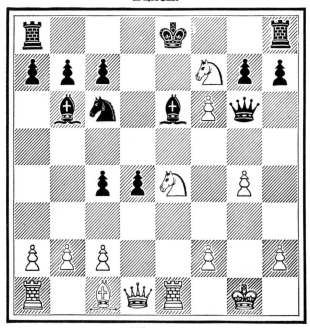

WHITE.

| 13. | . . . . . . | Castles |
|-----|-------------|---------|

Now, at once, all of the White pieces become badly placed, and must speedily return to their camp. The tide turns and the reaction sets in.

| 14. | KKt—Kt5 | B—Q4 |
|-----|---------|------|
| 15. | P×P | KR—K |
| 16. | Kt—Kt3 | P—KR3 |
| 17. | Kt—R3 | Kt—K4 |

and Black should win; or, perhaps more effectively,

| 17. | . . . . . . | R×R |
| 18. | Q×R | R—K |
| 19. | Q—Q | Kt—K4 |
| 20. | Kt—B4 | Q—B3 |

with a brilliant attack.

| 1. | P—K4 | P—K4 |
| 2. | Kt—KB3 | Kt—QB3 |
| 3. | P—QB3 | |

The Ponziani opening. I cannot recommend it to you on account of the questionable early advance of the QB Pawn which it involves.

| 3. | . . . . . . | P—Q4 |

An excellent answer. By his third move White has weakened the square Q3; so Black tries to open the Q file, to get possession of that very important point.

| 4. | Q—R4 | P×P |
| 5. | Kt×P | Q—Q4 |
| 6. | B—Kt5 | KKt—K2 |
| 7. | P—KB4 | |

This is the move given by Staunton. It is intended to keep up the attack, which by the exchange of the minor pieces would be utterly lost. White threatens now B—B4, and Staunton lets Black, therefore, reply by P×P *e. p.* A fine Liverpool player, looking at the position with the instinct of a true Chess player, thought that there must be, against such precipitate attack as White has undertaken, a better reply. And this is how he defeated one of his opponents in a match game.

| 7. | . . . . . . | B—Q2 |
| 8. | Kt×B | K×Kt |
| 9. | Castles | Kt—B4 |

Black has by far the better development, and now threatens B—B4ch.

| | White | Black |
|---|---|---|
| 10. | P—QKt4 | P—QR4 |
| 11. | K—R | P×P |
| 12. | B×Ktch. | P×B |
| 13. | Q×R | B—B4 |
| 14. | Q×R | Kt—Kt6ch. |
| 15. | P×Kt | Q—R4checkmate. |

| | WHITE. | BLACK. |
|---|---|---|
| | Blackburne. | Burn. |
| 1. | P—K4 | P—K3 |
| 2. | P—Q4 | P—Q4 |
| 3. | Kt—QB3 | Kt—KB3 |
| 4. | P—K5 | KKt—Q2 |
| 5. | P—B4 | P—QB4 |
| 6. | P×P | B×P |
| 7. | Q—Kt4 | Castles |
| 8. | B—Q3 | P—B4 |
| 9. | Q—R3 | Kt—QB3 |
| 10. | Kt—B3 | R—K |

Black is evidently preparing his K side for a long siege. His last move answers that purpose excellently. The Rook vacates the square KB for the Kt, which is there quite secure, and gives his support to the weakest point, the KRP, besides to K3 and to Kt3, and is always ready to obstruct the KKt file.

| | | |
|---|---|---|
| 11. | P—KKt4 | P—KKt3 |
| 12. | P—QR3 | |

One of those harmless looking moves, to prevent something that really is no threat at all. Those superfluous defensive moves spoil many a game. Why not at once Q—Kt3, and then a vigorous advance of the KRP?

| 12. | . . . . . . | P—QR3 |
| 13. | B—Q2 | P—QKt4 |
| 14. | P×P | KtP×P |
| 15. | Castles QR | Kt—B |
| 16. | KR—Ktch. | |

A bold and promising sacrifice, which yields a violent attack very difficult to meet.

| 16. | . . . . . . | B×R |
| 17. | R×Bch. | Kt—Kt3 |
| 18. | Kt—K2 | R—R2 |

Again an excellent defensive manœuvre. The Rook protects several of the weakest points, and can be used as a means of obstructing the open KKt file.

| 19. | Kt—Kt3 | KR—K2 |
| 20. | Kt—R5 | K—R |
| 21. | Kt—B6 | R—KKt2 |
| 22. | Q—R6 | Kt—B |
| 23. | Kt—Kt5 | |

Black is practically out of danger, but must yet play very carefully. White intends now to continue with (24) Q×Rch., R×Q; (25) Kt—B7ch., R×Kt; (26) R—Kt8 mate.

| 23. | . . . . . . | R—Kt3 |
| 24. | Q—R5 | QR—KKt2 |
| 25. | R—Kt3 | Q—K2 |

Another protection to the KRP. White's attack slackens down because his two Bishops cannot find an opening to add their weight to it.

| 26. | B—K2 | R×Kt(B3) |

vigorous and decisive.

| 27. | P×R | Q×BP |
|-----|------|------|
| 28. | R—QB3 | B—Q2 |
| 29. | Kt—B3 | K—Kt |

White threatened R×Kt, followed by B—QB3.

| 30. | Q—R3 | Kt—Kt3 |
|-----|------|------|
| 31. | Q—R6 | Q—K2 |
| 32. | R×Kt | B×R |

A last attempt to neutralize Black's material superiority by attack.

| 33. | B—B3 | R—B2 |
|-----|------|------|
| 34. | Kt—Kt5 | Kt×P |
| 35. | Kt×R | Kt×Bch. |
| 36. | K—Q2 | Kt×B |

and Black won after a few more moves.

BLACK.—Steinitz.

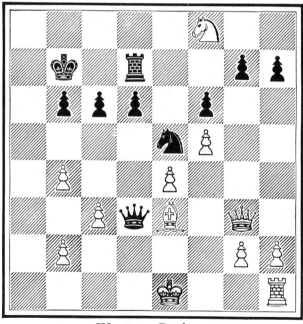

WHITE.—Lasker.

The annexed position occurred in my match with Mr. Steinitz; White to move. I played somewhat hastily.

### 1.   R—B

being under the impression that Kt×R would lead to a draw by perpetual check. This is, however (as, I believe, first pointed out by Tschigorin), not the case, e. g., (1) Kt×R, Q—Kt8ch.; (2) K—Q2, Q×Pch.; (3) K—Q, Q—Kt6ch.; (4) K—K2, Q—B5ch.; (5) K—K! Q×Pch.; (6) B—Q2, Q—R8ch.; (7) K—K2, and White should easily win.

| 1. | . . . . . . | Q—B7 |
| 2. | B—Q2 | R—K2 |
| 3. | Kt—K6 | Q×Pch. |

Here White must be extremely careful in selecting his reply. If he plays the plausible (4) K—Q, Q—Kt8ch.; (5) B—B, Kt—Q6; (6) Q×QP, Kt×Pch.; (7) K—K2, Q—K4ch.; (8) B—K3, Q×Bch., equalizing the material forces, and with good chances for a draw.

### 4.   Q—K3          Q×KtP

Now follows a very important manœuvre, the key to White's defence.

### 5.   P—Kt3

If (5) Q—K2 instead, Black will answer by Q—Q4, and have all the Q side at his own disposal

### 5.   . . . . . .          R—K

To take the RP would not be sufficient to keep the balance of forces; White would reply with K—Q or P—Kt5, and very soon be able to assume the attack.

6.  Q—K2        Q—R6

The first symptom of the gradual exhaustion of Black's attack. The Q would be better posted somewhere on the Q side; but Q—Q4 is not playable, as P—B4 would now force the exchange of Queens.

7.  K—Q        R—QR

8.  R—B2      R—R7

Black's pieces are well placed, but they do not threaten anything.

9.   P—Kt5     P—B4

10.  Kt×KtP   P—Q4

11.  K—B

White threatens to drive the Rook away, in order to bring matters speedily to a climax.

11.  ......       Q—Q6

(11) ...., P—B5 would be answered by (12) P×P, (11) ...., Kt—Q6ch. by K—Kt; and the resulting exchanges leave White always in the possession of his advantage.

12.  Q×Q       Kt×Qch.

13.  K—Kt       R—Kt7ch.

14.  K—R        R×P

15.  R—B3

and White won the ending.

BLACK.—Lasker.

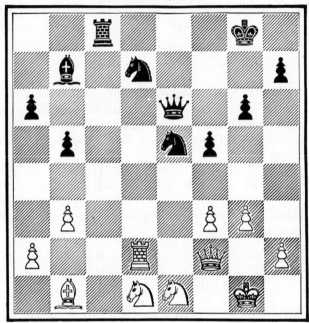

WHITE.—Steinitz.

This diagram shows the state of the game No. 18, at move 33, White to play, of my match with Mr. Steinitz. I recommend you the careful study of this position, in which White can keep the balance only by a very ingenious manœuvre of defence. The question concerns *only* the next move of White. Black threatens (1) ...., Kt×Pch.; (2) Kt×Kt, B×Kt; (3) Q×B, Q—K8ch., winning.

How is White to save his game?

If (1) R—B2, R×R; (2) B×R, Q—B3; (3)

K—Kt2, Kt×P; (4) Kt×Kt, Kt—K4, will regain the piece and keep the Pawn plus.

If (1) R—K2, R—B8; (2) B—B2, Q—Q4; (3) Kt—K3, Q×BP, or else (3) R—Q2, Kt×Pch.; (4) Kt×Kt, Q×Kt; (5) Q×Q, B×Q; (6) R× Kt, R×B, should win. (1) Kt—K3 may be answered by (1) ...., R—B8; (2) R—Q, Kt× Pch.; (3) Kt×Kt, R×Rch.; (4) Kt×R, Q—Q4, again remaining a Pawn ahead, with at least an even position.

If (1) K—Kt2, Kt×P; (2) Kt×Kt, Kt—K4; (3) R—Q3, R—B8; (4) R—Q8ch., K—Kt2; (5) Q—R7, Q—B3, will yield an irresistible attack to the second player.

The move actually made, and the only one to save the game (which ended in a draw) was (1) K—B! against which Black must play very cautiously not to be at a disadvantage; any too violent attack will fail.

You will have sometimes to look very deep into the position to find a good move for the defence. But this much, I believe, I can promise you, that if you follow the rules laid down you will not search in vain. If you will seek, you will find, no matter how dangerous the attack may look.

## Nos. 10, 11, 12

Gentlemen: When both parties through the struggles of the middle game have held their own, when by the exertions undergone in attack and defence the material forces on both sides have become decimated, and direct attacks on the King have consequently lost any chance of success, the game enters upon a new stage, differing in many points from those preceding it. Of this part of the game, called the end game, it is a characteristic that the King—hitherto the direct or indirect object of attack on the part of your opponent—over whose safety you anxiously watched, and whose power was limited to the protection of a few Pawns needed for his own security, now becomes a powerful weapon of offence and aggression in your hands.

When the game enters this last stage, the general rules for attack and defence are not changed in any particular. Weaknesses will principally be represented by Pawns, which are blocked, or cannot advance for some other reason, and which, besides, cannot be defended by other Pawns. Here again the attack will direct itself against the weaknesses. Our weak points will be such as are open to the enemy's men or King, and not commanded by any of our own men nor by our King; our opponent's weak points will be directed toward those strong points, and will attempt to create new ones as near the hostile weaknesses as it has the power to do. Here also the attacking party needs, for success, a superiority of some kind. But, in combination with all this, two new factors enter into the end game which give it its peculiar character.

The first is based on the greater facility acquired (in consequence of the exhaustion of the material forces) to lead your passed Pawns to Queen. For that purpose there are never more than five separate moves required, and often less. If the line where the Pawn advances consists entirely of strong points, the enemy will be obliged to engage one of his men, perhaps his King, whose function it will be to command one of these points or to obstruct that line. Points and lines through which the hostile men prevent the advance of the passed Pawn may be called *points of vantage* in regard to it. The game will very often then present a fight for the command of these points or lines of advance, which may be intercepted by our men, or from which the hostile forces may be driven back. On the other hand, being quite satisfied with the result that part of the hostile army is engaged in watching our passed Pawn, we may undertake an attack with all our forces in some other quarter.

When attack and defence in the very latest stages of the game are so evenly balanced, and both our own men and those of our opponent are so favorably placed, that, unless the adversary voluntarily gives way, neither party can improve his position; when, in other words, the move ceases to be a privilege, "time" (the right to move, that is, to do something useful), will assume a new and very different character. In such positions as are very frequent in well contested games,

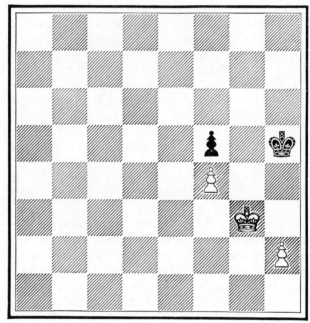

and the occurrence of which can often with certainty be forecalculated, to have to move means often a *loss* in the working power of your pieces, and it may consequently lose you the game. We shall speak of this as the *principle of exhaustion* (that is, exhaustion of moves to *improve* your position). This principle will manifest itself in the great care with which the two combatants hold back certain moves, which either would improve their position, or at least not affect it harmfully, until a favorable opportunity has arrived for executing them.

The principle of exhaustion may be illustrated by the diagrams.

White, manœuvring on the KR or KKt file, has no chance to force the win; there is not sufficient space at his disposal. For instance, after (1) K—R3, K—R3; (2) K—R4, K—Kt3, he would have to recede; therefore we must leave that quarter of the board to the Black King. Our KRP will consequently be a weakness, and it will be wise to hold it back as long as possible. The best position for the Black King to occupy will be Kt5. Whenever he will occupy that, our King must be ready to march to K3 or K5. From this we deduce the following line of play:

| | | |
|---|---|---|
| 1. | K—R3 | K—R3 |
| 2. | K—Kt2 | K—R4 |
| 3. | K—Kt3 | K—R3 |

the first manifestation of the principle.

| | | |
|---|---|---|
| 4. | K—B2 | K—R4 |
| 5. | K—K2 | |

Not (5) K—K3, as (5) ...., K—Kt5 would win a Pawn.

| | | |
|---|---|---|
| 5. | ...... | K—R5 |
| 6. | K—Q3 | K—Kt5 |
| 7. | K—K3 | K—R6 |
| 8. | K—Q4 | K×P |
| 9. | K—K5 winning | |

BLACK.

WHITE.

White has two chances of winning, the one based on his passed Pawn, the other on the weakness of the Black RP. The Black K occupies at present a position of advantage in regard to both. This is changed by the following manœuvre:

| | | |
|---|---|---|
| 1. | K—Q5 | K—B |
| 2. | K—B4 | K—Q |
| 3. | K—Q4 | K—B |
| 4. | K—Q5 | K—B2 |
| 5. | K—B5 | |

BLACK.

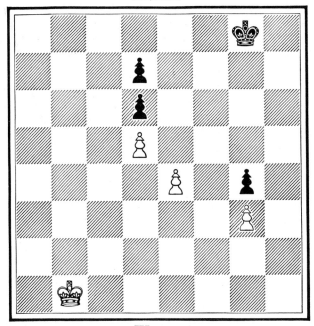

WHITE.

Now the move is changed, and White wins easily;
or,

| 4. | . . . . . . | K—Q |
|---|---|---|
| 5. | K—Q6 | K—B |
| 6. | P—B7 | K—Kt2 |
| 7. | K—Q7 | |

and mates in a few more moves.

An ending by Mr. Locock (page 109).

White has two dangerous attacks; the one
against the weak Black KKtP, the K threatening

it from KB4; the object of the other is to advance
his P—K5, supported by the K at Q4. Therefore, when the White King will be at K3, the
Black K must be able to occupy in that moment
KKt4; and when the White King will stand on
Q4, the Black King must prevent the threatened
advance by marching to KB3. If then the White
King is at Q3, ready to go in one move to either
of these squares, the hostile King must stand on
Kt3. Thus, the different squares on each side
correspond to each other. This mode of reasoning followed up, we shall come to the conclusion
that White with the move draws, Black with the
move loses.

For example, if Black moves first,

|  |  |  |
|---|---|---|
| 1. | ...... | K—R |
| 2. | K—Kt2 | K—Kt |
| 3. | K—Kt3 | K—R2 |
| 4. | K—B2 | K—R3 |
| 5. | K—Q2 | K—R4 |
| 6. | K—B3 | K—Kt4 |
| 7. | K—B4 | K—Kt3 |
| 8. | K—Q3 | K—Kt4 |
| 9. | K—K3 and wins; or | |
| 8. | ...... | K—B3 |
| 9. | K—Q4 | K—Kt3 |
| 10. | P—K5 | P×Pch. |
| 11. | K×P | K—B2 |
| 12. | K—B5 winning | |

Now let White have the move.

|  |  |  |
|---|---|---|
| 1. | K—B2 | K—R2 |
| 2. | K—Q2 | K—R3 |

| 3. | K—K2 | K—R4 |
| 4. | K—Q2 | K—R3 |
| 5. | K—B2 | K—R2 |
| 6. | K—B3 | K—Kt2 |
| 7. | K—B4 | K—B2 |
| 8. | K—Q4 | K—B3 |
| 9. | K—Q3 | K—Kt3 |
| 10. | K—K3 | K—Kt4, etc. |

One of the gentlemen present, Mr. McLaren, asked for the explanation of following position:

BLACK.

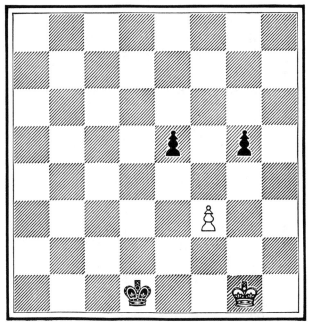

WHITE.

This position depends also on the principle of exhaustion. Black's points of advantage, from where he attacks the White Pawn, are three—K7, K6, KB5. The most forward and, therefore, best of these is K7. Whenever the Black King is there, the White King must be ready to occupy KKt2; and whenever the Black King marches to K6, the White King must take the point KKt3. The game will run therefore—

| 1. | K—R | K—Q7 |
|---|---|---|
| 2. | K—R2 | K—Q6 |
| 3. | K—R3 | K—Q5 |
| 4. | K—Kt4 | K—K6 |
| 5. | K—Kt3 | K—K7 |
| 6. | K—Kt2 | K—Q8 |
| 7. | K—R (or R3) and draws | |

An attempt to force one of the passed Pawns will fail.

| 1. | K—R | P—Kt5 |
|---|---|---|
| 2. | K—Kt2, and draws | |

Black with the move will win.

| 1. | . . . . . . | K—K8 |
|---|---|---|
| 2. | K—Kt2 | K—K7 |
| 3. | K—Kt3 | K—B8 |
| 4. | K—R3 | K—B7 |
| 5. | K—Kt4 | K—Kt7 winning |

The following positions are illustrative of the power of the passed Pawn:

BLACK.

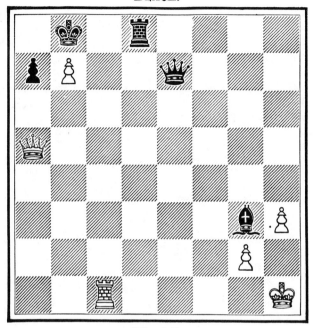

WHITE.

White wins by a clever stroke, in which all the powers of the Pawn at Kt7 are made use of.

    1.  R—B8ch.        R×R
    2.  Q×Pch.        K×Q
    P×R, becomes a Kt, wins the Q and the game.

The above is more of a mid game combination than an end game type; but even backed by very little force, a passed Pawn can be very dangerous.

BLACK.

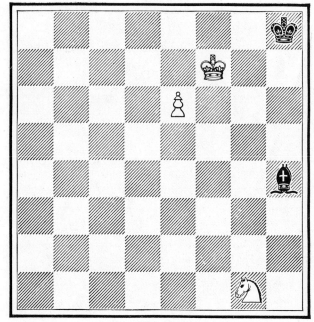

WHITE.

| | 1. | Kt—B3 | B—Q |
|---|---|---|---|
| | 2. | Kt—K5 | K—R2 |
| | 3. | Kt—Kt4 | K—R |
| | 4. | Kt—B6 | |

and wins, as Black has to move; if (3) ...., B—
R5 (Kt4); (4) Kt—B6ch. would obstruct the
Bishop file and therefore win.

**115**

WHITE.

| 1. | B—Q4 | B—Kt6 |
|----|-------|-------|
| 2. | B—R7 | B—B5 |
| 3. | B—Kt8 | B—K6 |
| 4. | B—B7 | B—R7 |
| 5. | B—Kt6 | |

and wins in a few more moves. In both of the latter cases the King of the winning party is exceedingly well placed.

BLACK.

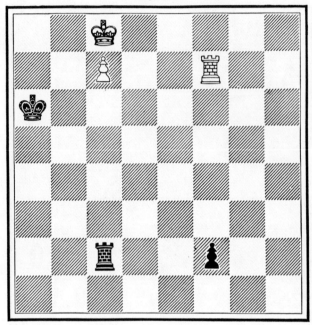

WHITE.

The difference in the position of the Kings decides the struggle.

| 1. | K—Kt8 | R—Kt7ch. |
| 2. | K—R8 | R—B7 |
| 3. | R—B6ch. | K—R4 |

If K—Kt4, (4), K—Kt8 would speedily win.

| 4. | K—Kt8 | R—Kt7ch. |
| 5. | K—R7 | R—B7 |

| | | |
|---|---|---|
| 6. | R—B5ch. | K—R5 |
| 7. | K—Kt7 | R—Kt7ch. |
| 8. | K—R6 | R—B7 |
| 9. | R—B4ch. | K—R6 |
| 10. | K—Kt6 | R—Kt7ch. |
| 11. | K—R5 | R—B7 |
| 12. | R—B3ch. | K—R7 |
| 13. | R×P | |

and wins by Queen against Rook.

BLACK.

WHITE.

| 1. | . . . . . . | R—Kt7ch. |
|---|---|---|
| 2. | K—B | R—Kt5 |
| 3. | P becomes a Rook | |

If P Queens instead, R—B5ch., sacrificing itself, would force the stalemate.

| 3. | . . . . . . | R—QR5 |
|---|---|---|
| 4. | R—QR8 | K—Kt5 |

An excellent move. White threatened P—R6—R7, and then a check with his Rook. If now (5) P—R6, K—B6, threatening Mate, will force the draw, for instance, (6) K—K, K—K6; (7) K—Q, K—Q6; (8) K—B, K—B6; (9) K—Kt, R—Kt5ch., and so on

| 5. | K—K2 | K—B4 |
|---|---|---|
| 6. | P—R6 | K—B3 |

not K—K3, as (7) P—R7, K—Q2; (8) R—KR8 would gain the Rook.

| 7. | K—Q3 | |

The decisive manœuvre. The King comes now to the support of the Pawn, in order to liberate the Rook, while Black can do nothing to change the position to his advantage. The square QR7 is left free for the King, to allow him a place of safety against the checks of the Black Rook.

| 7. | . . . . . . | K—Kt2 |
|---|---|---|
| 8. | K—B3 | K—R2 |
| 9. | K—Kt3 | R—R4 |
| 10. | K—Kt4 | R—R8 |
| 11. | K—Kt5 | R—Kt8ch. |
| 12. | K—B6 | R—B8ch. |
| 13. | K—Kt7 | R—Kt8ch. |
| 14. | K—R7 | |

Without this place of refuge the game would never be won. Now it is a very simple matter.

| 14. | ...... | K—Kt2 |
|-----|--------|-------|
| 15. | R—Kt8 | R—QR8 |
| 16. | R—Kt6 | K—B2 |
| 17. | K—Kt7 winning easily. | |

BLACK.

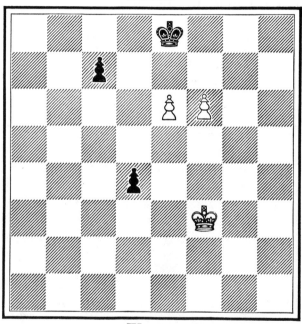

WHITE.

Here White wins by his superior K position and because his Pawns are further advanced than those of Black.

     1.   K—B4

It is necessary to time the winning manœuvre correctly. Therefore we must not at once march to K4.

| 1. | ...... | K—B |
| 2. | K—K4 | P—B4 |
| 3. | K—Q3 | K—K |
| 4. | P—K7 | |

The right moment for the advance. Now all Black's movements are forced.

| 4. | ...... | K—Q2 |
| 5. | K—B4 | K—K |
| 6. | K×P | P—Q6 |
| 7. | K—Q6 | P—Q7 |
| 8. | K—K6 | P Queens |
| 9. | P—B7checkmate | |

BLACK.

WHITE.

1.  P—QR5          B—R3

The White QRP has only to pass one more Black Square, and that within two moves; therefore the Bishop must hurry to stop it.

2.  P—Kt5ch.      B×P

Now the Bishop is obstructed by his own King.

3.  K—K4          B—R5
4.  K—B3

and the Pawn will Queen.

When the end game stage is nearing, the power of the various pieces is altered to a marked degree. Different issues being at stake, different measures must be adopted, and ideas, correct in the early part of the game, become sensibly modified. The value of each piece varies, of course, with each end game position in a greater or lesser degree; but the men have a certain average value, which will serve as guide. This value will be determined—

  (a) By their fighting capacity against the adverse King as an aggressive piece,
  (b) and against passed Pawns,
  (c) and finally their *reach* or power of offence, when obstructions (as is usual in end games) are few.

Let us first consider the King. Being placed in opposition to the adverse King, he will take three squares from him, and can thus hinder him from advancing. He can, single-handed, stop three united passed Pawns, not advanced beyond the sixth row; and two, one of which is on the seventh row. He can attack every square on the board, and that, if he is in a central point, for instance, at K4, in no more than three moves.

His reach is totally uninfluenced by obstructions other than the natural limits of the board. He is, therefore, a powerful weapon, if well developed in one of the central points or near important points; he can, however, never be used as an instrument of obstruction, never be exposed to any direct attack, which sensibly diminishes his offensive value against strong pieces of offence.

BLACK.—Morphy.

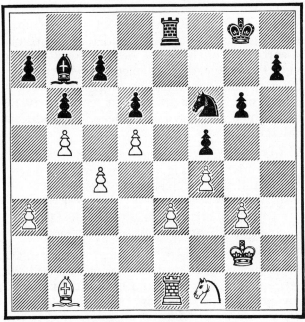

WHITE.—Harrwitz.

The annexed position occurred in one of Morphy's match games. The game went on:

| 1. | ...... | P—QR3 |
| 2. | P—R4 | P×P |
| 3. | RP×P | R—R |

The first advantage, an unopposed open file for the Rook, is now established.

| 4. | Kt—Q2 | R—R6 |
| 5. | P—K4 | P×P |
| 6. | Kt×P | Kt×Kt |
| 7. | B×Kt | R—QB6 |
| 8. | B—B3 | |

threatening now, of course, R—K8ch.—QKt8.

| 8. | ...... | K—B2 |
| 9. | R—K4 | B—B |
| 10. | B—K2 | B—B4 |
| 11. | R—Q4 | P—R4 |

Through this last move the important point at KB4 becomes strong.

| 12. | K—B2 | K—B3 |
| 13. | R—Q2 | B—B7 |
| 14. | K—K | B—K5 |
| 15. | K—B2 | K—B4 |

The White King is kept back by the Black Rook; the Black King, however, can advance unchecked.

| 16. | R—R2 | P—R5 |

forcing the way for his King, which will soon become a dangerous assailant.

| 17. | P×P | K×P |
| 18. | R—R7 | R—KR6 |
| 19. | R×P | R—R7ch. |
| 20. | K—K | K—K6 |

crushing every resistance.

BLACK.—Steinitz.

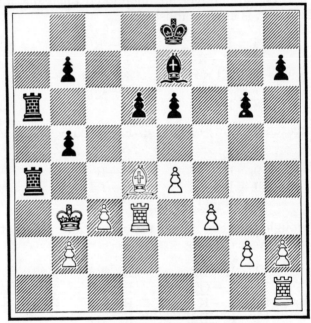

WHITE.—Lasker.

In one of my match games with Mr. Steinitz the above position occurred, White to move.

1.  K—RQ          P—K4

If K—Q2 at once, P—KB4 will give White a good game.

| | | |
|---|---|---|
| 2. | B—K3 | K—Q2 |
| 3. | B—B5 | R—R8 |
| 4. | KR—Q2 | K—K3 |
| 5. | B—R3 | P—Kt4 |
| 6. | R—Q5 | R—Kt3 |
| 7. | K—Kt4 | |

Now the King actively enters into the fight.

| | | |
|---|---|---|
| 7. | ...... | P—Kt5 |

The initiation of a subtle counter-attack which nearly succeeded in turning the tables.

| | | |
|---|---|---|
| 8. | K—R5 | ...... |

It might have been wiser first to accept the offered Pawn, thus: (8) P×P, R—K8; (9) K—R5, B—Q; (10) R×P, R—R3ch.; (11) K—Kt4, R×Pch.; (12) K—Kt3 remaining a Pawn ahead.

| | | |
|---|---|---|
| 8. | ...... | R—R3ch. |
| 9. | K×P | P—R4 |

(or 9) ...., R—R8; (10) P×P, R—K8; (11) P—R3, R×P; (12) P—B4.

| | | |
|---|---|---|
| 10. | R—Q | R×R |
| 11. | R×R | P×P |
| 12. | P×P | R—R |
| 13. | K—Kt6 | R—KKt |
| 14. | K×P | R—Kt7 |
| 15. | P—R4 | R—R7 |
| 16. | K—B6 | |

This manœuvre makes the Black game untenable.

| 16. | ...... | B×P |
| 17. | R×Pch. | K—B2 |
| 18. | K—Q5 | B—B3 |

If (18) ...., R—Q7ch.; (19) K×P, B—Kt6ch.; (20) P—B4, R×R; (21) B×R, P—R5; (22) B—B5, P—R6; (23) B—Kt and the four passed Pawns win easily against the Bishop.

| 19. | R—Q7ch. | K—Kt3 |
| 20. | K—K6 | |

to check the advance of the Black King.

If now (20) ...., K—Kt4; (21) R—KB7; B—Q; (22) R—B8, B—Kt3; (23) B—K7ch., K—Kt3; (24) R—Kt8ch., K—R2; (25) K—B7 followed by B—B6 would draw the Black King into a mating net.

| 20. | ...... | P—R5 |
| 21. | R—Q | P—R6 |
| 22. | R—Ktch. | R—Kt7 |
| 23. | R×Rch. | P×R |
| 24. | B—B5 | |

and wins after a few more moves with his passed Pawns.

BLACK.

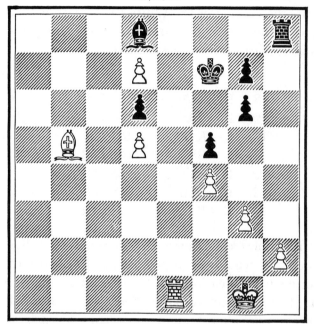

WHITE.—Morphy.

Another of Morphy's energetic end game attacks.

| | | |
|---|---|---|
| 1. | R—K8 | R—B |
| 2. | K—B2 | P—Kt4 |
| 3. | K—K3 | P—Kt5 |
| 4. | K—Q3 | P—Kt4 |
| 5. | B—B6 | P×P |
| 6. | P×P | R—Kt |
| 7. | K—B4 | |

The Black forces being all engaged by the combined action of the White Rook, passed Pawn and Bishop, the co-operation of the King is all that is necessary to decide the day.

| 7. | ...... | R—B |
|---|---|---|
| 8. | K—Kt5 | R—Kt |
| 9. | K—R6 | R—B |
| 10. | K—Kt7 | R—Kt |
| 11. | K—B8 | B—Kt3 |
| 12. | R×R | K×R |
| 13. | P Queens | B×Q |
| 14. | K×B | Resigns |

Examples concerning the power of the King could be readily multiplied. But we leave this for a future occasion, the King as an assailant, or as strong protective power being an essential element, yea, almost an organic part of each approximately even end game.

Another piece whose power increases the more the end game stage is approaching is the Rook. His fighting capacity against the adverse King is enormous, and exactly what makes him a valuable instrument for attack as well as defence. In conjunction with his own King he can checkmate the hostile K driven to the edge of the board, and in combination with a Kt and P and a single obstruction he can give checkmate to the K on any square of the board (example, Rook at B8, Kt at Kt6, P at B5; opponent's King at B7, one of his Pawns at Kt7).

Without any kind of support he can give untold checks to the adverse King, until the same is obliged to approach the Rook, perhaps against the best interests of his game, or forced to protect himself behind some kind of obstruction. On account of his attacking qualities, he is always a valuable ally when you want to force any obstructions out of the way, for instance, of passed Pawns; but he is less fit for fighting against them, and really too valuable a piece to be given away for such a purpose, if other alternatives are open. The best way to stop an adverse passed Pawn with a Rook is to place the Rook behind it, as his reach will increase the more the Pawn advances. He can stop and even win (if they are unsupported) two passed Pawns, of which one is on the sixth, the other on the fifth, row; but two passed Pawns on the sixth row will Queen against him if united. Used against advanced Pawns he is, therefore, not as manageable as the King, or even the Bishop, but he is the more dangerous to the Pawns before they assume a threatening attitude, as his reach is very great, and exactly calculated to serve against Pawns in their strongest position—that is, when they are abreast. He can attack, if unobstructed, any square of the board in one move, and will command thirteen at a time. This enables him to restrict the opposite King to a portion of the board.

This Bishop is very much less fit for assault against the King, or for restricting his approach, than the Rook. The Bishop can take away two squares from the King, and eventually give check and command two squares of the reach of the King. His capacity for yielding support to passed Pawns is not very great, as the line in which the Pawn advances will usually contain some points where obstructions are totally safe against him. His great value consists in two things: (1) That he can stop adverse Pawns from a long distance and from a number of squares. (2) That a Pawn and a Bishop may protect each other, so as to make both of them comparatively safe against the King or superior pieces. His chess-board, however, contains only thirty-two squares, and whichever influence they may have on the issue of the game, very much determines his share in it; so that his importance may be exaggerated when you have the superiority of position, or almost annihilated when the opposite is the case.

The Knight is, unless circumstances are very favorable, the weakest piece of all. He may take two squares from the King, or give check, and besides take away one square from him;

but the adverse King may approach him then, and get rid of him if no support is near. His great power is that he cannot be obstructed. When obstructions abound, and when he can occupy a strong point near the enemy's line, he can be an invaluable ally. His reach never exceeds eight points, situated in a circle, and he may be obliged to take five moves to cross the board from one point to another (for instance, the two diagonally opposite corner points). On an extended field of battle he must, therefore, choose the wing to which he will give his support, or very much lose in value.

To refer to the oft mooted question, "Which piece is stronger, the Bishop or the Knight?" it is clear that the value of the Bishop undergoes greater changes than that of the Knight. If experience has shown that, on an average, during the opening or middle game, the Bishop will be at least as strong as the Knight, this will be the more true the more obstructions disappear, that is, in endings with only a few Pawns scattered about the board. In complicated end game positions, where Pawns partly form blocks, the Knight will find his best chance. The value of two Bishops varies, of course, as they dominate the whole chess-board, very much less than that of one; in consequence, two Bishops are, as a rule, appreciably stronger than two Kts or a Bishop and a Kt.

BLACK.

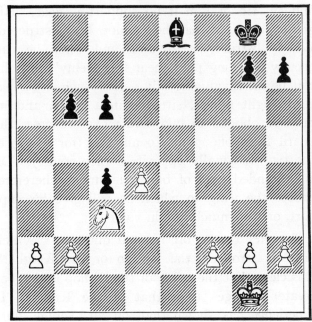

WHITE.

From a correspondence game.

1.  Kt—K4          P—QKt4
2.  P—QR3

Now all the Black squares on the Q side are in

possession of White; nor can this be changed, as the Black King is necessary on the K side to fight against the White Pawns.

| 2. | ...... | B—Kt3 |
|----|--------|-------|
| 3. | P—B3 | K—B2 |
| 4. | K—B2 | K—K3 |
| 5. | K—K3 | P—R3 |
| 6. | P—KKt4 | K—Q4 |
| 7. | Kt—B3ch. | K—Q3 |
| 8. | P—B4 | B—K |

It would have been more advisable to keep the Bishop in the rear of the advancing Pawns.

| 9. | P—B5 | B—Q2 |
|----|------|------|
| 10. | Kt—K4ch. | K—K2 |

If (10) ...., K—Q4; (11) P—B6 will force the exchange of Kt v. B. and the extra Pawn will easily win.

| 11. | K—B4 | B—K |
|-----|------|-----|
| 12. | K—K5 | B—B2 |
| 13. | P—KR4 | B—Q4 |
| 14. | P—Kt5 | P×P |
| 15. | P×P | B—Kt |
| 16. | P—Kt6 | Resigns |

as P—B6 will soon prove decisive.

BLACK.

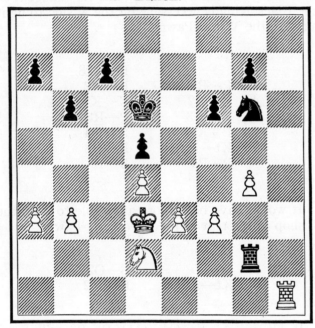

WHITE.

From another game by correspondence.

Black to move.

1.  ......          P—QB4

Strong, and embarrassing to White. The
Pawn engages the QP, which is the only White
piece that commands the point K5. It can, therefore, not take the hostile Pawn, as after (2) P×
Pch., P×P, White has no means to stop the

check at K4, which would soon prove fatal to him.

    2.  R—R7

unsatisfactory enough; but the Kt cannot move to any square improving his position, and without exposing the White Pawns to the attack of the Rook.

| 2. | . . . . . . | P×P |
|----|-------------|------|
| 3. | P×P | Kt—B5ch. |
| 4. | K—B3 | Kt—K3 |

Now White can do nothing effectual. If the Rook moves, Black will win the QP.

| 5. | K—Q3 | P—QR4 |
|----|------|-------|
| 6. | K—K3 | R—Kt8 |

This manœuvre with the Rook is splendid. He threatens now R—QB8—B6ch. winning the QP. White cannot frustrate that plan, *e. g.*, (7) K—Q3, R—QB8; (8) P—R4, Kt—B5ch.; (9) K—K3, P—KKt4; (10) K—B2, R—Q8, etc.

| 7. | R—R8 | R—QB8 |
|----|------|-------|
| 8. | R—QKt8 | R—B6ch. |
| 9. | K—B2 | Kt×P |
| 10. | R×Pch. | K—K4 |
| 11. | R—Kt7 | K—B5· |

If now (12) R×P, R—B7; (13) K—K, K—K6; (14) R—K7ch., K—Q6; (15) Kt—B, Kt×Pch.; (16) K—Q, P—Q5, and White has no satisfactory move left.

    12.  P—Kt5        R—K6

and White resigns, for after (13) P×P, P×P, (14) R—KB7, P—B4, his position becomes altogether untenable.

The following position occurred in a match game at Hastings, 1895, between Messrs. Schlechter and Tschigorin.

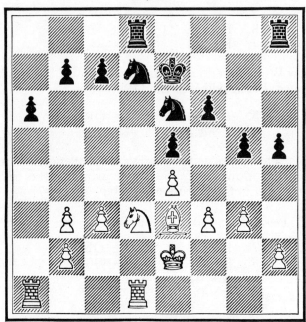

WHITE.

It was White's turn to move, and the game went on.

1.　P—QKt4

A Pawn move without a clearly defined purpose is to be blamed. The P at Kt4 takes away
a good square from the Kt, which that piece
ought to have occupied at once in order to
threaten Kt—Q5, and to force the advance P—
QB3, which would greatly increase the strength
of the B. Moreover, it leaves a strong point at
QB5 to the Black Kts, which White can only
guard by another advance of a Pawn.

| | |
|---|---|
| 1. ...... | R(Q)—KKt |
| 2. R—KKt | |

He ought not to leave the important Q file with
his Rook. All defensive purposes could be served
just as well by (2) P—KR3, which would enable
him to reply to (2) ...., P—Kt5 with (3) BP×
P, P×P, (4) P—R4 and to (2) ...., P—R5
with P—Kt4.

| | |
|---|---|
| 2. ...... | P—Kt5 |
| 3. P—KB4 | Kt—Q |
| 4. P—B5 | Kt—B2 |
| 5. Kt—B2 | Kt—Q3 |
| 6. B—B5 | Kt—Kt3 |

Not (6) ...., Kt×B, as (7) P×Kt, Kt moves
(8) P—B6 would follow.

| | |
|---|---|
| 7. Kt—Q | |

Now, decidedly, R—Q was at the right place,
when, for instance, (7) ...., R—Q; (8) R×
Kt, R×R; (9) R—Q would lead to a probable
draw.

| | |
|---|---|
| 7. ...... | Kt(Kt3)—B |
| 8. Kt—K3 | K—B2 |

Now the KP has become indefensible.

| | | |
|---|---|---|
| 9. | Kt—Q5 | P—B3 |
| 10. | Kt—B7 | Kt×KP |
| 11. | QR—Q | Kt×B |
| 12. | P×Kt | R—Q |
| 13. | Kt—K6 | R×R |
| 14. | R×R | K—K2 |
| 15. | P—R4 | |

In thus opening up files for the Black Rook he plays Black's game, (15) P—B4 is by far preferable. Neither the Black Kt nor the R will then ever be able to obtain good positions. (15) ...., P—R5 could then, for instance, be answered by (16) P×P; R×P; (17) R—Q8, Kt—R2; (18) R—QR8 winning the piece.

| | | |
|---|---|---|
| 15. | ...... | P×P e. p. |
| 16. | R—KR | K—B2 |
| 17. | R×P | Kt—K2 |
| 18. | P—KKt4 | P—R5 |
| 19. | P—B4 | Kt—Kt3 |

A pretty little move which threatens Kt—B.

| | | |
|---|---|---|
| 20. | P×Ktch. | K×Kt |
| 21. | P—Kt7 | R—KKt |
| 22. | R×P | R×P |
| 23. | K—K3 | K—B2 |

It remains to force the exchange of the last P on the K side, in order to have there all lines free, and a clear superiority.

| | | |
|---|---|---|
| 24. | P—Kt4 | K—Kt3 |

If the plausible (24) ...., K—Kt instead, then (25) K—K4, R—R2; (26) R×R, K×R;

(27)K—B5, K—Kt2; (28) P—KKt5, P×P;
(29) K×KtP, drawing without difficulty.

| | | |
|---|---|---|
| 25. | R—R8 | P—B4 |
| 26. | P×Pch. | K×P |
| 27. | R—R5ch. | . . . . . . |

(27) R—B8ch. would find its reply in K—K3;
(28) R—K8ch., K—Q2; (29) R×P, R—Kt6ch.;
(30) K moves R—QKt6, when Black will remain
with a winning advantage.

| | | |
|---|---|---|
| 27. | . . . . . . | K—K3 |
| 28. | R—R6ch. | K—Q2 |
| 29. | P—Kt5 | RP×P |
| 30. | P×P | P×P |
| 31. | K—K4 | R—K2 |
| 32. | R—QKt6 | K—B2 |
| 33. | R×P | K—B3 |
| 34. | R—R5 | R—K |

This manœuvre with the Rook, which wins a
move, decides the game. The White King dare
not move, as otherwise the Black KP advances
still further; so all White's moves are forced.

| | | |
|---|---|---|
| 35. | R—R7 | R—K3 |
| 36. | R—R5 | R—K2 |
| 37. | R—R | K×P |
| 38. | R—Bch. | K—Q3 |
| 39. | R—Qch. | K—B3 |
| 40. | R—Bch. | K—Q2 |
| 41. | R—B5 | K—Q3 |
| 42. | R—B2 | P—QKt4 |
| 43. | R—QKt2 | K—B4 |

and White resigned the struggle which Black had
masterfully conducted.

THE END.

CATALOGUE OF DOVER BOOKS

# Puzzles, Mathematical Recreations

**SYMBOLIC LOGIC and THE GAME OF LOGIC, Lewis Carroll.** "Symbolic Logic" is not concerned with modern symbolic logic, but is instead a collection of over 380 problems posed with charm and imagination, using the syllogism, and a fascinating diagrammatic method of drawing conclusions. In "The Game of Logic" Carroll's whimsical imagination devises a logical game played with 2 diagrams and counters (included) to manipulate hundreds of tricky syllogisms. The final section, "Hit or Miss" is a lagniappe of 101 additional puzzles in the delightful Carroll manner. Until this reprint edition, both of these books were rarities costing up to $15 each. Symbolic Logic: Index. xxxi + 199pp. The Game of Logic: 96pp. 2 vols. bound as one. 5⅜ x 8. T492 Paperbound **$1.50**

**PILLOW PROBLEMS and A TANGLED TALE, Lewis Carroll.** One of the rarest of all Carroll's works, "Pillow Problems" contains 72 original math puzzles, all typically ingenious. Particularly fascinating are Carroll's answers which remain exactly as he thought them out, reflecting his actual mental process. The problems in "A Tangled Tale" are in story form, originally appearing as a monthly magazine serial. Carroll not only gives the solutions, but uses answers sent in by readers to discuss wrong approaches and misleading paths, and grades them for insight. Both of these books were rarities until this edition, "Pillow Problems" costing up to $25, and "A Tangled Tale" $15. Pillow Problems: Preface and Introduction by Lewis Carroll. xx + 109pp. A Tangled Tale: 6 illustrations. 152pp. Two vols. bound as one. 5⅜ x 8. T493 Paperbound **$1.50**

**AMUSEMENTS IN MATHEMATICS, Henry Ernest Dudeney.** The foremost British originator of mathematical puzzles is always intriguing, witty, and paradoxical in this classic, one of the largest collections of mathematical amusements. More than 430 puzzles, problems, and paradoxes. Mazes and games, problems on number manipulation, unicursal and other route problems, puzzles on measuring, weighing, packing, age, kinship, chessboards, joiners', crossing river, plane figure dissection, and many others. Solutions. More than 450 illustrations. vii + 258pp. 5⅜ x 8. T473 Paperbound **$1.25**

**THE CANTERBURY PUZZLES, Henry Dudeney.** Chaucer's pilgrims set one another problems in story form. Also Adventures of the Puzzle Club, the Strange Escape of the King's Jester, the Monks of Riddlewell, the Squire's Christmas Puzzle Party, and others. All puzzles are original, based on dissecting plane figures, arithmetic, algebra, elementary calculus and other branches of mathematics, and purely logical ingenuity. "The limit of ingenuity and intricacy," The Observer. Over 110 puzzles. Full Solutions. 150 illustrations. vii + 225pp. 5⅜ x 8. T474 Paperbound **$1.25**

**MATHEMATICAL EXCURSIONS, H. A. Merrill.** Even if you hardly remember your high school math, you'll enjoy the 90 stimulating problems contained in this book and you will come to understand a great many mathematical principles with surprisingly little effort. Many useful shortcuts and diversions not generally known are included: division by inspection, Russian peasant multiplication, memory systems for pi, building odd and even magic squares, square roots by geometry, dyadic systems, and many more. Solutions to difficult problems. 50 illustrations. 145pp. 5⅜ x 8. T350 Paperbound **$1.00**

**MAGIC SQUARES AND CUBES, W. S. Andrews.** Only book-length treatment in English, a thorough non-technical description and analysis. Here are nasik, overlapping, ·pandiagonal, serrated squares; magic circles, cubes, sphe.es, rhombuses. Try your hand at 4-dimensional magical figures! Much unusual folklore and tradition included. High school algebra is sufficient. 754 diagrams and illustrations. viii + 419pp. 5⅜ x 8. T658 Paperbound **$1.85**

**CALIBAN'S PROBLEM BOOK: MATHEMATICAL, INFERENTIAL AND CRYPTOGRAPHIC PUZZLES, H. Phillips (Caliban), S. T. Shovelton, G. S. Marshall.** 105 ingenious problems by the greatest living creator of puzzles based on logic and inference. Rigorous, modern, piquant; reflecting their author's unusual personality, these intermediate and advanced puzzles all involve the ability to reason clearly through complex situations; some call for mathematical knowledge, ranging from algebra to number theory. Solutions. xi + 180pp. 5⅜ x 8. T736 Paperbound **$1.25**

**MATHEMATICAL PUZZLES FOR BEGINNERS AND ENTHUSIASTS, G. Mott-Smith.** 188 mathematical puzzles based on algebra, dissection of plane figures, permutations, and probability, that will test and improve your powers of inference and interpretation. The Odic Force, The Spider's Cousin, Ellipse Drawing, theory and strategy of card and board games like tit-tat-toe, go moku, salvo, and many others. 100 pages of detailed mathematical explanations. Appendix of primes, square roots, etc. 135 illustrations. 2nd revised edition. 248pp. 5⅜ x 8. T198 Paperbound **$1.00**

**MATHEMAGIC, MAGIC PUZZLES, AND GAMES WITH NUMBERS, R. V. Heath.** More than 60 new puzzles and stunts based on the properties of numbers. Easy techniques for multiplying large numbers mentally, revealing hidden numbers magically, finding the date of any day in any year, and dozens more. Over 30 pages devoted to magic squares, triangles, cubes, circles, etc. Edited by J. S. Meyer. 76 illustrations. 128pp. 5⅜ x 8. T110 Paperbound **$1.00**

# CATALOGUE OF DOVER BOOKS

**MATHEMATICAL RECREATIONS, M. Kraitchik.** One of the most thorough compilations of unusual mathematical problems for beginners and advanced mathematicians. Historical problems from Greek, Medieval, Arabic, Hindu sources. 50 pages devoted to pastimes derived from figurate numbers, Mersenne numbers, Fermat numbers, primes and probability. 40 pages of magic, Euler, Latin, panmagic squares. 25 new positional and permutational games of permanent value: fairy chess, latruncles, reversi, jinx, ruma, lasca, tricolor, tetrachrome, etc. Complete rigorous solutions. Revised second edition. 181 illustrations. 333pp. 5⅜ x 8.
T163 Paperbound **$1.75**

**MATHEMATICAL PUZZLES OF SAM LOYD, selected and edited by M. Gardner.** Choice puzzles by the greatest American puzzle creator and innovator. Selected from his famous collection, "Cyclopedia of Puzzles," they retain the unique style and historical flavor of the originals. There are posers based on arithmetic, algebra, probability, game theory, route tracing, topology, counter, sliding block, operations research, geometrical dissection. Includes the famous "14-15" puzzle which was a national craze, and his "Horse of a Different Color" which sold millions of copies. 117 of his most ingenious puzzles in all, 120 line drawings and diagrams. Solutions. Selected references. xx + 167pp. 5⅜ x 8. T498 Paperbound **$1.00**

**MATHEMATICAL PUZZLES OF SAM LOYD, Vol. II, selected and edited by Martin Gardner.** The outstanding 2nd selection from the great American innovator's "Cyclopedia of Puzzles": speed and distance problems, clock problems, plane and solid geometry, calculus problems, etc. Analytical table of contents that groups the puzzles according to the type of mathematics necessary to solve them. 166 puzzles, 150 original line drawings and diagrams. Selected references. xiv + 177pp. 5⅜ x 8. T709 Paperbound **$1.00**

**ARITHMETICAL EXCURSIONS: AN ENRICHMENT OF ELEMENTARY MATHEMATICS, H. Bowers and J. Bowers.** A lively and lighthearted collection of facts and entertainments for anyone who enjoys manipulating numbers or solving arithmetical puzzles: methods of arithmetic never taught in school, little-known facts about the most simple numbers, and clear explanations of more sophisticated topics; mysteries and folklore of numbers, the "Hin-dog-abic" number system, etc. First publication. Index. 529 numbered problems and diversions, all with answers. Bibliography. 60 figures. xiv + 320pp. 5⅜ x 8. T770 Paperbound **$1.65**

**CRYPTANALYSIS, H. F. Gaines.** Formerly entitled ELEMENTARY CRYPTANALYSIS, this introductory-intermediate level text is the best book in print on cryptograms and their solution. It covers all major techniques of the past, and contains much that is not generally known except to experts. Full details about concealment, substitution, and transposition ciphers; periodic mixed alphabets, multafid, Kasiski and Vigenere methods, Ohaver patterns, Playfair, and scores of other topics. 6 language letter and word frequency appendix. 167 problems, now furnished with solutions. Index. 173 figures. vi + 230pp. 5⅜ x 8.
T97 Paperbound **$2.00**

**CRYPTOGRAPHY, L. D. Smith.** An excellent introductory work on ciphers and their solution, the history of secret writing, and actual methods and problems in such techniques as transposition and substitution. Appendices describe the enciphering of Japanese, the Baconian biliteral cipher, and contain frequency tables and a bibliography for further study. Over 150 problems with solutions. 160pp. 5⅜ x 8. T247 Paperbound **$1.00**

**PUZZLE QUIZ AND STUNT FUN, J. Meyer.** The solution to party doldrums. 238 challenging puzzles, stunts and tricks. Mathematical puzzles like The Clever Carpenter, Atom Bomb; mysteries and deductions like The Bridge of Sighs, The Nine Pearls, Dog Logic; observation puzzles like Cigarette Smokers, Telephone Dial; over 200 others including magic squares, tongue twisters, puns, anagrams, and many others. All problems solved fully. 250pp. 5⅜ x 8.
T337 Paperbound **$1.00**

**101 PUZZLES IN THOUGHT AND LOGIC, C. R. Wylie, Jr.** Brand new problems you need no special knowledge to solve! Take the kinks out of your mental "muscles" and enjoy solving murder problems, the detection of lying fishermen, the logical identification of color by a blindman, and dozens more. Introduction with simplified explanation of general scientific method and puzzle solving. 128pp. 5⅜ x 8. T367 Paperbound **$1.00**

**MY BEST PROBLEMS IN MATHEMATICS, Hubert Phillips ("Caliban").** Only elementary mathematics needed to solve these 100 witty, catchy problems by a master problem creator. Problems on the odds in cards and dice, problems in geometry, algebra, permutations, even problems that require no math at all—just a logical mind, clear thinking. Solutions completely worked out. If you enjoy mysteries, alerting your perceptive powers and exercising your detective's eye, you'll find these cryptic puzzles a challenging delight. Original 1961 publication. 100 puzzles, solutions. x + 107pp. 5⅝ x 8. T91 Paperbound **$1.00**

**MY BEST PUZZLES IN LOGIC AND REASONING, Hubert Phillips ("Caliban").** A new collection of 100 inferential and logical puzzles chosen from the best that have appeared in England, available for first time in U.S. By the most endlessly resourceful puzzle creator now living. All data presented are both necessary and sufficient to allow a single unambiguous answer. No special knowledge is required for problems ranging from relatively simple to completely original one-of-a-kinds. Guaranteed to please beginners and experts of all ages. Original publication. 100 puzzles, full solutions. x + 107pp. 5⅜ x 8. T119 Paperbound **$1.00**

# CATALOGUE OF DOVER BOOKS

**THE BOOK OF MODERN PUZZLES, G. L. Kaufman.** A completely new series of puzzles as fascinating as crossword and deduction puzzles but based upon different principles and techniques. Simple 2-minute teasers, word labyrinths, design and pattern puzzles, logic and observation puzzles — over 150 braincrackers. Answers to all problems. 116 illustrations. 192pp. 5⅜ x 8.
T143 Paperbound **$1.00**

**NEW WORD PUZZLES, G. L. Kaufman.** 100 ENTIRELY NEW puzzles based on words and their combinations that will delight crossword puzzle, Scrabble and Jotto fans. Chess words, based on the moves of the chess king; design-onyms, symmetrical designs made of synonyms; rhymed double-crostics; syllable sentences; addle letter anagrams; alphagrams; linkograms; and many others all brand new. Full solutions. Space to work problems. 196 figures. vi + 122pp. 5⅜ x 8.
T344 Paperbound **$1.00**

**MAZES AND LABYRINTHS: A BOOK OF PUZZLES, W. Shepherd.** Mazes, formerly associated with mystery and ritual, are still among the most intriguing of intellectual puzzles. This is a novel and different collection of 50 amusements that embody the principle of the maze: mazes in the classical tradition; 3-dimensional, ribbon, and Möbius-strip mazes; hidden messages; spatial arrangements; etc.—almost all built on amusing story situations. 84 illustrations. Essay on maze psychology. Solutions. xv + 122pp. 5⅜ x 8.
T731 Paperbound **$1.00**

**MAGIC TRICKS & CARD TRICKS, W. Jonson.** Two books bound as one. 52 tricks with cards, 37 tricks with coins, bills, eggs, smoke, ribbons, slates, etc. Details on presentation, misdirection, and routining will help you master such famous tricks as the Changing Card, Card in the Pocket, Four Aces, Coin Through the Hand, Bill in the Egg, Afghan Bands, and over 75 others. If you follow the lucid exposition and key diagrams carefully, you will finish these two books with an astonishing mastery of magic. 106 figures. 224pp. 5⅜ x 8. T909 Paperbound **$1.00**

**PANORAMA OF MAGIC, Milbourne Christopher.** A profusely illustrated history of stage magic, a unique selection of prints and engravings from the author's private collection of magic memorabilia, the largest of its kind. Apparatus, stage settings and costumes; ingenious ads distributed by the performers and satiric broadsides passed around in the streets ridiculing pompous showmen; programs; decorative souvenirs. The lively text, by one of America's foremost professional magicians, is full of anecdotes about almost legendary wizards: Dede, the Egyptian; Philadelphia, the wonder-worker; Robert-Houdin, "the father of modern magic;" Harry Houdini; scores more. Altogether a pleasure package for anyone interested in magic, stage setting and design, ethnology, psychology, or simply in unusual people. A Dover original. 295 illustrations; 8 in full color. Index. viii + 216pp. 8⅜ x 11¼.
T774 Paperbound **$2.25**

**HOUDINI ON MAGIC, Harry Houdini.** One of the greatest magicians of modern times explains his most prized secrets. How locks are picked, with illustrated picks and skeleton keys; how a girl is sawed into twins; how to walk through a brick wall — Houdini's explanations of 44 stage tricks with many diagrams. Also included is a fascinating discussion of great magicians of the past and the story of his fight against fraudulent mediums and spiritualists. Edited by W.B. Gibson and M.N. Young. Bibliography. 155 figures, photos. xv + 280pp. 5⅜ x 8.
T384 Paperbound **$1.25**

**MATHEMATICS, MAGIC AND MYSTERY, Martin Gardner.** Why do card tricks work? How do magicians perform astonishing mathematical feats? How is stage mind-reading possible? This is the first book length study explaining the application of probability, set theory, theory of numbers, topology, etc., to achieve many startling tricks. Non-technical, accurate, detailed! 115 sections discuss tricks with cards, dice, coins, knots, geometrical vanishing illusions, how a Curry square "demonstrates" that the sum of the parts may be greater than the whole, and dozens of others. No sleight of hand necessary! 135 illustrations. xii + 174pp. 5⅜ x 8.
T335 Paperbound **$1.00**

**EASY-TO-DO ENTERTAINMENTS AND DIVERSIONS WITH COINS, CARDS, STRING, PAPER AND MATCHES, R. M. Abraham.** Over 300 tricks, games and puzzles will provide young readers with absorbing fun. Sections on card games; paper-folding; tricks with coins, matches and pieces of string; games for the agile; toy-making from common household objects; mathematical recreations; and 50 miscellaneous pastimes. Anyone in charge of groups of youngsters, including hard-pressed parents, and in need of suggestions on how to keep children sensibly amused and quietly content will find this book indispensable. Clear, simple text, copious number of delightful line drawings and illustrative diagrams. Originally titled "Winter Nights Entertainments." Introduction by Lord Baden Powell. 329 illustrations. v + 186pp. 5⅜ x 8½.
T921 Paperbound **$1.00**

**STRING FIGURES AND HOW TO MAKE THEM, Caroline Furness Jayne.** 107 string figures plus variations selected from the best primitive and modern examples developed by Navajo, Apache, pygmies of Africa, Eskimo, in Europe, Australia, China, etc. The most readily understandable, easy-to-follow book in English on perennially popular recreation. Crystal-clear exposition; step-by-step diagrams. Everyone from kindergarten children to adults looking for unusual diversion will be endlessly amused. Index. Bibliography. Introduction by A. C. Haddon. 17 full-page plates. 960 illustrations. xxiii + 401pp. 5⅜ x 8½.
T152 Paperbound **$2.00**

# Chess, Checkers, Games, Go

**THE ADVENTURE OF CHESS, Edward Lasker.** A lively history of chess, from its ancient beginnings in the Indian 4-handed game of Chaturanga, through to the great players of our day, as told by one of America's finest masters. He introduces such unusual sidelights and amusing oddities as Maelzel's chess-playing automaton that beat Napoleon 3 times. Major discussion of chess-playing machines and personal memories of Nimzovich, Capablanca, etc. 5-page chess primer. 11 illustrations, 53 diagrams. 296pp. 5⅜ x 8. S510 Paperbound **$1.45**

**A TREASURY OF CHESS LORE, edited by Fred Reinfeld.** A delightful collection of anecdotes, short stories, aphorisms by and about the masters, poems, accounts of games and tournaments, photography. Hundreds of humorous, pithy, satirical, wise, and historical episodes, comments, and word portraits. A fascinating "must" for chess players; revealing and perhaps seductive to those who wonder what their friends see in the game. 48 photographs (14 full page plates) 12 diagrams. xi + 306pp. 5⅜ x 8. T458 Paperbound **$1.75**

**HOW DO YOU PLAY CHESS? by Fred Reinfeld.** A prominent expert covers every basic rule of chess for the beginner in 86 questions and answers: moves, powers of pieces, rationale behind moves, how to play forcefully, history of chess, and much more. Bibliography of chess publications. 11 board diagrams. 48 pages. **FREE**

**THE PLEASURES OF CHESS, Assiac.** Internationally known British writer, influential chess columnist, writes wittily about wide variety of chess subjects: Anderssen's "Immortal Game;" only game in which both opponents resigned at once; psychological tactics of Reshevsky, Lasker; varieties played by masters for relaxation, such as "losing chess;" sacrificial orgies; etc. These anecdotes, witty observations will give you fresh appreciation of game. 43 problems. 150 diagrams. 139pp. 5⅜ x 8. T597 Paperbound **$1.25**

**WIN AT CHESS, F. Reinfeld.** 300 practical chess situations from actual tournament play to sharpen your chess eye and test your skill. Traps, sacrifices, mates, winning combinations, subtle exchanges, show you how to WIN AT CHESS. Short notes and tables of solutions and alternative moves help you evaluate your progress. Learn to think ahead playing the "crucial moments" of historic games. 300 diagrams. Notes and solutions. Formerly titled CHESS QUIZ. vi + 120pp. 5⅜ x 8. T438 Paperbound **$1.00**

**THE ART OF CHESS, James Mason.** An unabridged reprinting of the latest revised edition of the most famous general study of chess ever written. Also included, a complete supplement by Fred Reinfeld, "How Do You Play Chess?", invaluable to beginners for its lively question and answer method. Mason, an early 20th century master, teaches the beginning and intermediate player more than 90 openings, middle game, end game, how to see more moves ahead, to plan purposefully, attack, sacrifice, defend, exchange, and govern general strategy. Supplement. 448 diagrams. 1947 Reinfeld-Bernstein text. Bibliography. xvi + 340pp. 5⅜ x 8. T463 Paperbound **$1.85**

**THE PRINCIPLES OF CHESS, James Mason.** This "great chess classic" (N. Y. Times) is a general study covering all aspects of the game: basic forces, resistance, obstruction, opposition, relative values, mating, typical end game situations, combinations, much more. The last section discusses openings, with 50 games illustrating modern master play of Rubinstein, Spielmann, Lasker, Capablanca, etc., selected and annotated by Fred Reinfeld. Will improve the game of any intermediate-skilled player, but is so forceful and lucid that an absolute beginner might use it to become an accomplished player. 1946 Reinfeld edition. 166 diagrams. 378pp. 5⅜ x 8. T646 Paperbound **$1.85**

**LASKER'S MANUAL OF CHESS, Dr. Emanuel Lasker.** Probably the greatest chess player of modern times, Dr. Emanuel Lasker held the world championship 28 years, independent of passing schools or fashions. This unmatched study of the game, chiefly for intermediate to skilled players, analyzes basic methods, combinations, position play, the aesthetics of chess, dozens of different openings, etc., with constant reference to great modern games. Contains a brilliant exposition of Steinitz's important theories. Introduction by Fred Reinfeld. Tables of Lasker's tournament record. 3 indices. 308 diagrams. 1 photograph. xxx + 349pp. 5⅜ x 8. T640 Paperbound **$2.00**

**THE ART OF CHESS COMBINATION, E. Znosko-Borovsky.** Proves that combinations, perhaps the most aesthetically satisfying, successful technique in chess, can be an integral part of your game, instead of a haphazard occurrence. Games of Capablanca, Rubinstein, Nimzovich, Bird, etc. grouped according to common features, perceptively analyzed to show that every combination begins in certain simple ideas. Will help you to plan many moves ahead. Technical terms almost completely avoided. "In the teaching of chess he may claim to have no superior," P. W. Sergeant. Introduction. Exercises. Solutions. Index. 223pp. 5⅜ x 8. T583 Paperbound **$1.45**

# CATALOGUE OF DOVER BOOKS

**MODERN IDEAS IN CHESS, Richard Reti.** An enduring classic, because of its unrivalled explanation of the way master chess had developed in the past hundred years. Reti, who was an outstanding theoretician and player, explains each advance in chess by concentrating on the games of the single master most closely associated with it: Morphy, Anderssen, Steinitz, Lasker, Alekhine, other world champions. Play the games in this volume, study Reti's perceptive observations, and have a living picture of the road chess has travelled. Introduction. 34 diagrams. 192pp. 5⅜ x 8. T638 Paperbound **$1.25**

**THE BOOK OF THE NEW YORK INTERNATIONAL CHESS TOURNAMENT, 1924, annotated by A. Alekhine and edited by H. Helms.** Long a rare collector's item, this is the book of one of the most brilliant tournaments of all time, during which Capablanca, Lasker, Alekhine, Reti, and others immeasurably enriched chess theory in a thrilling contest. All 110 games played, with Alekhine's unusually penetrating notes. 15 photographs. xi + 271pp. 5⅜ x 8. T752 Paperbound **$1.85**

**KERES' BEST GAMES OF CHESS, selected, annotated by F. Reinfeld.** 90 best games, 1931-1948, by one of boldest, most exciting players of modern chess. Games against Alekhine, Bogolyubov, Capablanca, Euwe, Fine, Reshevsky, other masters, show his treatments of openings such as Giuoco Piano, Alekhine Defense, Queen's Gambit Declined; attacks, sacrifices, alternative methods. Preface by Keres gives personal glimpses, evaluations of rivals. 110 diagrams. 272pp. 5⅜ x 8. T593 Paperbound **$1.35**

**HYPERMODERN CHESS as developed in the games of its greatest exponent, ARON NIMZOVICH, edited by Fred Reinfeld.** An intensely original player and analyst, Nimzovich's extraordinary approaches startled and often angered the chess world. This volume, designed for the average player, shows in his victories over Alekhine, Lasker, Marshall, Rubinstein, Spielmann, and others, how his iconoclastic methods infused new life into the game. Use Nimzovich to invigorate your play and startle opponents. Introduction. Indices of players and openings. 180 diagrams. viii + 220pp. 5⅜ x 8. T448 Paperbound **$1.35**

**THE DEVELOPMENT OF A CHESS GENIUS: 100 INSTRUCTIVE GAMES OF ALEKHINE, F. Reinfeld.** 100 games of the chess giant's formative years, 1905-1914, from age 13 to maturity, each annotated and commented upon by Fred Reinfeld. Included are matches against Bogolyubov, Capablanca, Tarrasch, and many others. You see the growth of an inexperienced genius into one of the greatest players of all time. Many of these games have never appeared before in book form. "One of America's most significant contributions to the chess world," Chess Life. New introduction. Index of players, openings. 204 illustrations. xv +227pp. 5¾ x 8. T551 Paperbound **$1.35**

**RESHEVSKY'S BEST GAMES OF CHESS, Samuel Reshevsky.** One time 4-year-old chess genius, 5-time winner U. S. Chess Championship, selects, annotates 110 of his best games, illustrating theories, favorite methods of play against Capablanca, Alekhine, Bogolyubov, Kashdan, Vidmar, Botvinnik, others. Clear, non-technical style. Personal impressions of opponents, autobiographical material, tournament match record. Formerly "Reshevsky on Chess." 309 diagrams, 2 photos. 288pp. 5⅜ x 8. T606 Paperbound **$1.25**

**ONE HUNDRED SELECTED GAMES, Mikhail Botvinnik.** Author's own choice of his best games before becoming World Champion in 1948, beginning with first big tournament, the USSR Championship, 1927. Shows his great power of analysis as he annotates these games, giving strategy, technique against Alekhine, Capablanca, Euwe, Keres, Reshevsky, Smyslov, Vidmar, many others. Discusses his career, methods of play, system of training. 6 studies of endgame positions. 221 diagrams. 272pp. 5⅜ x 8. T620 Paperbound **$1.50**

**RUBINSTEIN'S CHESS MASTERPIECES, selected, annotated by Hans Kmoch.** Thoroughgoing mastery of opening, middle game; faultless technique in endgame, particularly rook and pawn endings; ability to switch from careful positional play to daring combinations; all distinguish the play of Rubinstein. 100 best games, against Janowski, Nimzowitch, Tarrasch, Vidmar, Capablanca, other greats, carefully annotated, will improve your game rapidly. Biographical introduction, B. F. Winkelman. 103 diagrams. 192pp. 5⅜ x 8. T617 Paperbound **$1.25**

**TARRASCH'S BEST GAMES OF CHESS, selected & annotated by Fred Reinfeld.** First definitive collection of games by Siegbert Tarrasch, winner of 7 international tournaments, and the leading theorist of classical chess. 183 games cover fifty years of play against Mason, Mieses, Paulsen, Teichmann, Pillsbury, Janwoski, others. Reinfeld includes Tarrasch's own analyses of many of these games. A careful study and replaying of the games will give you a sound understanding of classical methods, and many hours of enjoyment. Introduction. Indexes. 183 diagrams. xxiv + 386pp. 5⅜ x 8. T644 Paperbound **$2.00**

**MARSHALL'S BEST GAMES OF CHESS, F. J. Marshall.** Grandmaster, U. S. Champion for 27 years, tells story of career; presents magnificent collection of 140 of best games, annotated by himself. Games against Alekhine, Capablanca, Emanuel Lasker, Janowski, Rubinstein, Pillsbury, etc. Special section analyzes openings such as King's Gambit, Ruy Lopez, Alekhine's Defense, Giuoco Piano, others. A study of Marshall's brilliant offensives, slashing attacks, extraordinary sacrifices, will rapidly improve your game. Formerly "My Fifty Years of Chess." Introduction. 19 diagrams. 13 photos. 250pp. 5⅜ x 8. T604 Paperbound **$1.45**

# CATALOGUE OF DOVER BOOKS

**THE HASTINGS CHESS TOURNAMENT, 1895, edited by Horace F. Cheshire.** This is the complete tournament book of the famous Hastings 1895 tournament. One of the most exciting tournaments ever to take place, it evoked the finest play from such players as Dr. Lasker, Steinitz, Tarrasch, Harry Pillsbury, Mason, Tchigorin, Schlecter, and others. It was not only extremely exciting as an event, it also created first-rate chess. This book contains fully annotated all 230 games, full information about the playing events, biographies of the players, and much other material that makes it a chess classic. 22 photos, 174 diagrams. x + 370pp. 5⅝ x 8½. T288 Paperbound **$2.00**

**THE BOOK OF THE NOTTINGHAM INTERNATIONAL CHESS TOURNAMENT, 1936, Annotated by Dr. Alexander Alekhine.** The Nottingham 1936 tournament is regarded by many chess enthusiasts as the greatest tournament of recent years. It brought together all the living former world champions, the current chess champion, and the future world champion: Dr. Lasker, Capablanca, Alekhine, Euwe, Botvinnik, and Reshevsky, Fine, Flohr, Tartakover, Vidmar, and Bogoljubov. The play was brilliant throughout. This volume contains all 105 of the games played, provided with the remarkable annotations of Alekhine. 1 illustration, 121 diagrams. xx + 291pp. 5⅜ x 8½. T189 Paperbound **$1.85**

**CHESS FOR FUN AND CHESS FOR BLOOD, Edward Lasker.** A genial, informative book by one of century's leading masters. Incisive comments on chess as a form of art and recreation, on how a master prepares for and plays a tournament. Best of all is author's move-by-move analysis of his game with Dr. Emanuel Lasker in 1924 World Tournament, a charming and thorough recreation of one of the great games in history: the author's mental processes; how his calculations were upset; how both players blundered; the surprising outcome. Who could not profit from this study-in-depth? For the enthusiast who likes to read about chess as well as play it. Corrected (1942) edition. Preface contains 8 letters to author about the fun of chess. 95 illustrations by Maximilian Mopp. 224pp. 5⅜ x 8½. T146 Paperbound **$1.25**

**HOW NOT TO PLAY CHESS, Eugene A. Znosko-Borovsky.** Sticking to a few well-chosen examples and explaining every step along the way, an outstanding chess expositor shows how to avoid playing a hit-or-miss game and instead develop general plans of action based on positional analysis: weak and strong squares, the notion of the controlled square, how to seize control of open lines, weak points in the pawn structure, and so on. Definition and illustration of typical chess mistakes plus 20 problems (from master games) added by Fred Reinfeld for the 1949 edition and a number of good-to-memorize tips make this a lucid book that can teach in a few hours what might otherwise take years to learn. 119pp. 5⅜ x 8. T920 Paperbound **$1.00**

**THE SOVIET SCHOOL OF CHESS, A. Kotov and M. Yudovich.** 128 master games, most unavailable elsewhere, by 51 outstanding players, including Botvinnik, Keres, Smyslov, Tal, against players like Capablanca, Euwe, Reshevsky. All carefully annotated, analyzed. Valuable biographical information about each player, early history of Russian chess, careers and contributions of Chigorin and Alekhine, development of Soviet school from 1920 to present with full over-all study of main features of its games, history of Russian chess literature. The most comprehensive work on Russian chess ever printed, the richest single sourcebook for up-to-date Russian theory and strategy. New introduction. Appendix of Russian Grandmasters, Masters, Master Composers. Two indexes (Players, Games). 30 photographs. 182 diagrams. vi + 390pp. 5⅜ x 8. T26 Paperbound **$2.00**

**THE ART OF THE CHECKMATE, Georges Renaud and Victor Kahn.** Two former national chess champions of France examine 127 games, identify 23 kinds of mate, and show the rationale for each. These include Legal's pseudo sacrifice, the double check, the smothered mate, Greco's mate, Morphy's mate, the mate of two bishops, two knights, many, many more. Analysis of ideas, not memorization problems. Review quizzes with answers help readers gauge progress. 80 quiz examples and solutions. 299 diagrams. vi + 208pp. T106 Paperbound **$1.35**

**HOW TO SOLVE CHESS PROBLEMS, K. S. Howard.** Full of practical suggestions for the fan or the beginner—who knows only the moves of the chessmen. Contains preliminary section and 58 two-move, 46 three-move, and 8 four-move problems composed by 27 outstanding American problem creators in the last 30 years. Explanation of all terms and exhaustive index. "Just what is wanted for the student," Brian Harley. 112 problems, solutions. vi +171pp. 5⅜ x 8. T748 Paperbound **$1.00**

**CHESS STRATEGY, Edward Lasker.** Keres, Fine, and other great players have acknowledged their debt to this book, which has taught just about the whole modern school how to play forcefully and intelligently. Covers fundamentals, general strategic principles, middle and end game, objects of attack, etc. Includes 48 dramatic games from master tournaments, all fully analyzed. "Best textbook I know in English," J. R. Capablanca. New introduction by author. Table of openings. Index. 167 illustrations. vii + 282pp. 5⅜ x 8. T528 Paperbound **$1.50**

**REINFELD ON THE END GAME IN CHESS, F. Reinfeld.** Formerly titled PRACTICAL END-GAME PLAY, this book contains clear, simple analyses of 62 end games by such masters as Alekhine, Tarrasch, Marshall, Morphy, Capablanca, and many others. Primary emphasis is on the general principles of transition from middle play to end play. This book is unusual in analyzing weak or incorrect moves to show how error occurs and how to avoid it. Covers king and pawn, minor piece, queen endings, weak squares, centralization, tempo moves, and many other vital factors. 62 diagrams. vi + 177pp. 5⅜ x 8. T417 Paperbound **$1.25**

# CATALOGUE OF DOVER BOOKS

**THE AMERICAN TWO-MOVE CHESS PROBLEM, Kenneth S. Howard.** One of this country's foremost contemporary problem composers selects an interesting, diversified collection of the best two-movers by 58 top American composers. Involving complete blocks, mutates, line openings and closings, other unusual moves, these problems will help almost any player improve his strategic approach. Probably has no equal for all around artistic excellence, surprising keymoves, interesting strategy. Includes 30-page history of development of American two-mover from Loyd, its founder, to the present. Index of composers. vii + 99pp. 5⅜ x 8½.
T997 Paperbound **$1.00**

**WIN AT CHECKERS, M. Hopper.** (Formerly CHECKERS). The former World's Unrestricted Checker Champion discusses the principles cf the game, expert's shots and traps, problems for the beginner, standard openings, locating your best move, the end game, opening "blitzkrieg" moves, ways to draw when you are behind your opponent, etc. More than 100 detailed questions and answers anticipate your problems. Appendix. 75 problems with solutions and diagrams. Index. 79 figures. xi + 107pp. 5⅜ x 8.
T363 Paperbound **$1.00**

**GAMES ANCIENT AND ORIENTAL, AND HOW TO PLAY THEM, E. Falkener.** A connoisseur's selection of exciting and different games: Oriental varieties of chess, with unusual pieces and moves (including Japanese shogi); the original pachisi; go; reconstructions of lost Roman and Egyptian games; and many more. Full rules and sample games. Now play at home the games that have entertained millions, not on a fad basis, but for millennia. 345 illustrations and figures. iv + 366pp. 5⅜ x 8.
T739 Paperbound **$2.00**

**GO AND GO-MOKU, Edward Lasker.** A fascinating Oriental game, Go, is winning new devotees in America daily. Rules that you can learn in a few minutes—and a combinations that makes it more profound than chess! This is an easily followed step-by-step explanation of this 2000-year-old game, beginning with fundamentals. New chapter on advanced strategy in this edition! Also contains rules for Go-Moku, a very easy sister game. 72 diagrams. xix + 215pp. 5⅜ x 8.
T613 Paperbound **$1.50**

**HOW TO FORCE CHECKMATE, F. Reinfeld.** Formerly titled CHALLENGE TO CHESSPLAYERS, this is an invaluable collection of 300 lightning strokes selected from actual masters' play, which will demonstrate how to smash your opponent's game with strong decisive moves. No board needed — clear, practical diagrams and easy-to-understand solutions. Learn to plan up to three moves ahead and play a superior end game. 300 diagrams. 111pp. 5⅜ x 8.
T439 Paperbound **$1.25**

**CHESSBOARD MAGIC! A COLLECTION OF 160 BRILLIANT ENDINGS, I. Chernev.** Contains 160 endgame compositions, all illustrating not only ingenuity of composition, but inherent beauty of solution. In one, five Knights are needed to force mate; in another White forces stalemate though Black finishes eight passed pawns ahead; 150 more, all remarkable, all will sharpen your imagination and increase your skill. "Inexhaustible source of entertainment, an endless feast of delight," Reuben Fine, Grandmaster. Introduction. 160 diagrams. Index of composers. vii + 172pp. 5⅜ x 8.
T607 Paperbound **$1.00**

**LEARN CHESS FROM THE MASTERS, F. Reinfeld.** Formerly titled CHESS BY YOURSELF, this book contains 10 games which you play against such masters as Marshall, Bronstein, Najdorf, and others, and an easy system for grading each move you make against a variety of other possible moves. Detailed annotations reveal the principles of the game through actual play. 91 diagrams. viii + 144pp. 5⅜ x 8.
T362 Paperbound **$1.00**

**MORPHY'S GAMES OF CHESS, edited by Philip W. Sergeant.** You can put boldness into your game by following the brilliant, forceful moves of the man who has been called the greatest chess player of all time. Here are 300 of Morphy's best games carefully annotated to reveal Morphy's principles. 54 classics against masters like Anderssen, Harrwitz, Bird, Paulsen, and others. 52 games at odds; 54 blindfold games; plus over 100 others. Unabridged reissue of the latest revised edition. Bibliography. New introduction by Fred Reinfeld. Annotations and introduction by Sergeant. Index. 235 diagrams. x + 352pp. 5⅜ x 8.
T386 Paperbound **$1.85**

**CHESS PRAXIS, Aron Nimzovich.** Nimzovich was the stormy petrel of chess in the first decades of this century, and his system, known as hypermodern chess, revolutionized all play since his time. Casting aside the classical chess theory of Steinitz and Tarrasch, he created his own analysis of chess, considering dynamic patterns as they emerge during play. This is the fullest exposition of his ideas, and it is easily one of the dozen greatest books ever written on chess. Nimzovich illustrates each of his principles with at least two games, and shows how he applied his concepts successfully in games against such masters as Alekhine, Tarrasch, Reti, Rubinstein, Capablanca, Spielmann and others. Indispensable to every serious chess player. Translated by J. DuMont. 135 diagrams, 1 photo. xi + 364pp. 5½ x 8⅝.
T296 Paperbound **$2.00**

**CHESS AND CHECKERS: THE WAY TO MASTERSHIP, Edward Lasker.** Complete, lucid instructions for the beginner—and valuable suggestions for the advanced player! For both games the great master and teacher presents fundamentals, elementary tactics, and steps toward becoming a superior player. He concentrates on general principles rather than a mass of rules, comprehension rather than brute memory. Historical introduction. 118 diagrams. xiv + 167pp. 5⅜ x 8.
T657 Paperbound **$1.15**

# CATALOGUE OF DOVER BOOKS

# Fiction

**THE LAND THAT TIME FORGOT and THE MOON MAID, Edgar Rice Burroughs.** In the opinion of many, Burroughs' best work. The first concerns a strange island where evolution is individual rather than phylogenetic. Speechless anthropoids develop into intelligent human beings within a single generation. The second projects the reader far into the future and describes the first voyage to the Moon (in the year 2025), the conquest of the Earth by the Moon, and years of violence and adventure as the enslaved Earthmen try to regain possession of their planet. "An imaginative tour de force that keeps the reader keyed up and expectant," NEW YORK TIMES. Complete, unabridged text of the original two novels (three parts in each). 5 illustrations by J. Allen St. John. vi + 552pp. 5⅜ x 8½.
T1020 Clothbound **$3.75**
T358 Paperbound **$2.00**

**AT THE EARTH'S CORE, PELLUCIDAR, TANAR OF PELLUCIDAR: THREE SCIENCE FICTION NOVELS BY EDGAR RICE BURROUGHS.** Complete, unabridged texts of the first three Pellucidar novels. Tales of derring-do by the famous master of science fiction. The locale for these three related stories is the inner surface of the hollow Earth where we discover the world of Pellucidar, complete with all types of bizarre, menacing creatures, strange peoples, and alluring maidens—guaranteed to delight all Burroughs fans and a wide circle of adventure lovers. Illustrated by J. Allen St. John and P. F. Berdanier. vi + 433pp. 5⅜ x 8½.
T1051 Paperbound **$2.00**

**THREE MARTIAN NOVELS, Edgar Rice Burroughs.** Contains: Thuvia, Maid of Mars; The Chessmen of Mars; and The Master Mind of Mars. High adventure set in an imaginative and intricate conception of the Red Planet. Mars is peopled with an intelligent, heroic human race which lives in densely populated cities and with fierce barbarians who inhabit dead sea bottoms. Other exciting creatures abound amidst an inventive framework of Martian history and geography. Complete unabridged reprintings of the first edition. 16 illustrations by J. Allen St. John. vi + 499pp. 5⅜ x 8½.
T39 Paperbound **$1.85**

**TO THE SUN? and OFF ON A COMET!, Jules Verne.** Complete texts of two of the most imaginative flights into fancy in world literature display the high adventure that have kept Verne's novels read for nearly a century. Only unabridged edition of the best translation, by Edward Roth. Large, easily readable type. 50 illustrations selected from first editions. 462pp. 5⅜ x 8.
T634 Paperbound **$1.75**

**FROM THE EARTH TO THE MOON and ALL AROUND THE MOON, Jules Verne.** Complete editions of two of Verne's most successful novels, in finest Edward Roth translations, now available after many years out of print. Verne's visions of submarines, airplanes, television, rockets, interplanetary travel; of scientific and not-so-scientific beliefs; of peculiarities of Americans; all delight and engross us today as much as when they first appeared. Large, easily readable type. 42 illus. from first French edition. 476pp. 5⅜ x 8.
T633 Paperbound **$1.75**

**THREE PROPHETIC NOVELS BY H. G. WELLS, edited by E. F. Bleiler.** Complete texts of "When the Sleeper Wakes" (1st book printing in 50 years), "A Story of the Days to Come," "The Time Machine" (1st complete printing in book form). Exciting adventures in the future are as enjoyable today as 50 years ago when first printed. Predict TV, movies, intercontinental airplanes, prefabricated houses, air-conditioned cities, etc. First important author to foresee problems of mind control, technological dictatorships. "Absolute best of imaginative fiction," N. Y. Times. Introduction. 335pp. 5⅜ x 8.
T605 Paperbound **$1.50**

**SEVEN SCIENCE FICTION NOVELS, H. G. Wells.** Full unabridged texts of 7 science-fiction novels of the master. Ranging from biology, physics, chemistry, astronomy to sociology and other studies, Mr. Wells extrapolates whole worlds of strange and intriguing character. "One will have to go far to match this for entertainment, excitement, and sheer pleasure . . . ," NEW YORK TIMES. Contents: The Time Machine, The Island of Dr. Moreau, First Men in the Moon, The Invisible Man, The War of the Worlds, The Food of the Gods, In the Days of the Comet. 1015pp. 5⅜ x 8.
T264 Clothbound **$4.50**

**28 SCIENCE FICTION STORIES OF H. G. WELLS.** Two full unabridged novels, MEN LIKE GODS and STAR BEGOTTEN, plus 26 short stories by the master science-fiction writer of all time. Stories of space, time, invention, exploration, future adventure—an indispensable part of the library of everyone interested in science and adventure. PARTIAL CONTENTS: Men Like Gods, The Country of the Blind, In the Abyss, The Crystal Egg, The Man Who Could Work Miracles, A Story of the Days to Come, The Valley of Spiders, and 21 more! 928pp. 5⅜ x 8.
T265 Clothbound **$4.50**

**THE WAR IN THE AIR, IN THE DAYS OF THE COMET, THE FOOD OF THE GODS: THREE SCIENCE FICTION NOVELS BY H. G. WELLS.** Three exciting Wells offerings bearing on vital social and philosophical issues of his and our own day. Here are tales of air power, strategic bombing, East vs. West, the potential miracles of science, the potential disasters from outer space, the relationship between scientific advancement and moral progress, etc. First reprinting of "War in the Air" in almost 50 years. An excellent sampling of Wells at his storytelling best. Complete, unabridged reprintings. 16 illustrations. 645pp. 5⅜ x 8½.
T1135 Paperbound **$2.00**

# CATALOGUE OF DOVER BOOKS

**THE PIRATES OF VENUS and LOST ON VENUS: TWO VENUS NOVELS BY EDGAR RICE BURROUGHS.** Two related novels, complete and unabridged. Exciting adventure on the planet Venus with Earthman Carson Napier broken-field running through one dangerous episode after another. All lovers of swashbuckling science fiction will enjoy these two stories set in a world of fascinating societies, fierce beasts, 5000-ft. trees, lush vegetation, and wide seas. Illustrations by Fortunino Matania. Total of vi + 340pp. 5⅜ x 8½.     T1053 Paperbound **$1.75**

**A PRINCESS OF MARS and A FIGHTING MAN OF MARS: TWO MARTIAN NOVELS BY EDGAR RICE BURROUGHS.** "Princess of Mars" is the very first of the great Martian novels written by Burroughs, and it is probably the best of them all; it set the pattern for all of his later fantasy novels and contains a thrilling cast of strange peoples and creatures and the formula of Olympian heroism amidst ever-fluctuating fortunes which Burroughs carries off so successfully. "Fighting Man" returns to the same scenes and cities—many years later. A mad scientist, a degenerate dictator, and an indomitable defender of the right clash—with the fate of the Red Planet at stake! Complete, unabridged reprinting of original editions. Illustrations by F. E. Schoonover and Hugh Hutton. v + 356pp. 5⅜ x 8½.
    T1140 Paperbound **$1.75**

**RURITANIA COMPLETE: THE PRISONER OF ZENDA and RUPERT OF HENTZAU, Anthony Hope.** The first edition to include in one volume both the continually-popular "Prisoner of Zenda" and its equally-absorbing sequel. Hope's mythical country of Ruritania has become a household word and the activities of its inhabitants almost a common heritage. Unabridged reprinting. 14 illustrations by Charles Dana Gibson. vi + 414pp. 5⅜ x 8.
    T69 Paperbound **$1.35**

**FLATLAND, E. A. Abbott.** A science-fiction classic of life in a 2-dimensional world that is also a first-rate introduction to such aspects of modern science as relativity and hyperspace. Political, moral, satirical, and humorous overtones have made FLATLAND fascinating reading for thousands. 7th edition. New introduction by Banesh Hoffmann. 16 illustrations. 128pp. 5⅜ x 8.     T1 Paperbound **$1.00**

**THE WONDERFUL WIZARD OF OZ, L. F. Baum.** Only edition in print with all the original W. W. Denslow illustrations in full color—as much a part of "The Wizard" as Tenniel's drawings are for "Alice in Wonderland." "The Wizard" is still America's best-loved fairy tale, in which, as the author expresses it, "The wonderment and joy are retained and the heartaches and nightmares left out." Now today's young readers can enjoy every word and wonderful picture of the original book. New introduction by Martin Gardner. A Baum bibliography. 23 full-page color plates. viii + 268pp. 5⅜ x 8.     T691 Paperbound **$1.50**

**THE MARVELOUS LAND OF OZ, L. F. Baum.** This is the equally enchanting sequel to the "Wizard," containing the adventures of the Scarecrow and the Tin Woodman. The hero this time is a little boy named Tip, and all the delightful Oz magic is still present. This is the book with the Animated Saw-horse, the Woggle-Bug, and Jack Pumpkinhead. All the original John R. Neill illustrations, 16 in full color. 287pp. 5⅜ x 8.     T692 Paperbound **$1.50**

**FIVE GREAT DOG NOVELS, edited by Blanche Cirker.** The complete original texts of five classic dog novels that have delighted and thrilled millions of children and adults throughout the world with stories of loyalty, adventure, and courage. Full texts of Jack London's "The Call of the Wild"; John Brown's "Rab and His Friends"; Alfred Ollivant's "Bob, Son of Battle"; Marshall Saunders' "Beautiful Joe"; and Ouida's "A Dog of Flanders." 21 illustrations from the original editions. 495pp. 5⅜ x 8.     T777 Paperbound **$1.75**

**THE CASTING AWAY OF MRS. LECKS AND MRS. ALESHINE, F. R. Stockton.** A charming light novel by Frank Stockton, one of America's finest humorists (and author of "The Lady, or the Tiger?"). This book has made millions of Americans laugh at the reflection of themselves in two middle-aged American women involved in some of the strangest adventures on record. You will laugh, too, as they endure shipwreck, desert island, and blizzard with maddening tranquility. Also contains complete text of "The Dusantes," sequel to "The Casting Away." 49 original illustrations by F. D. Steele. vii + 142pp. 5⅜ x 8.     T743 Paperbound **$1.00**

**GHOST AND HORROR STORIES OF AMBROSE BIERCE, Selected and introduced by E. F. Bleiler.** 24 morbid, eerie tales—the cream of Bierce's fiction output. Contains such memorable pieces as "The Moonlit Road," "The Damned Thing," "An Inhabitant of Carcosa," "The Eyes of the Panther," "The Famous Gilson Bequest," "The Middle Toe of the Right Foot," and other chilling stories, plus the essay, "Visions of the Night" in which Bierce gives us a kind of rationale for his aesthetic of horror. New collection (1964). xxii + 199pp. 5⅜ x 8⅜.     T767 Paperbound **$1.00**

**BEST GHOST STORIES OF J. S. LE FANU, Selected and introduced by E. F. Bleiler.** LeFanu is deemed the greatest name in Victorian supernatural fiction. Here are 16 of his best horror stories, including 2 nouvelles: "Carmilla," a classic vampire tale couched in a perverse eroticism, and "The Haunted Baronet." Also: "Sir Toby's Will," "Green Tea," "Schalken the Painter," "Ultor de Lacy," "The Familiar," etc. The first American publication of about half of this material: a long-overdue opportunity to get a choice sampling of LeFanu's work. New selection (1964). 8 illustrations. 5⅜ x 8⅜.     T415 Paperbound **$1.85**

# Nature

**AN INTRODUCTION TO BIRD LIFE FOR BIRD WATCHERS, Aretas A. Saunders.** Fine, readable introduction to birdwatching. Includes a great deal of basic information on about 160 different varieties of wild birds—elementary facts not easily found elsewhere. Complete guide to identification procedures, methods of observation, important habits of birds, finding nests, food, etc. "Could make bird watchers of readers who never suspected they were vulnerable to that particular virus," CHICAGO SUNDAY TRIBUNE. Unabridged, corrected edition. Bibliography. Index. 22 line drawings by D. D'Ostilio. Formerly "The Lives of Wild Birds." 256pp. 5⅜ x 8½. **T1139 Paperbound $1.00**

**LIFE HISTORIES OF NORTH AMERICAN BIRDS, Arthur Cleveland Bent.** Bent's historic, all-encompassing series on North American birds, originally produced under the auspices of the Smithsonian Institution, now being republished in its entirety by Dover Publications. The twenty-volume collection forms the most comprehensive, most complete, most-used source of information in existence. Each study describes in detail the characteristics, range, distribution, habits, migratory patterns, courtship procedures, plumage, eggs, voice, enemies, etc. of the different species and subspecies of the birds that inhabit our continent, utilizing reports of hundreds of contemporary observers as well as the writings of the great naturalists of the past. Invaluable to the ornithologist, conservationist, amateur naturalist, and birdwatcher. All books in the series contain numerous photographs to provide handy guides for identification and study.

**LIFE HISTORIES OF NORTH AMERICAN BIRDS OF PREY.** Including hawks, eagles, falcons, buzzards, condors, owls, etc. Index. Bibliographies of 923 items. 197 full-page plates containing close to 400 photographs. Total of 907pp. 5⅜ x 8½.     Vol. I: T931 Paperbound **$2.50**
Vol. II: T932 Paperbound **$2.50**
The set Paperbound **$5.00**

**LIFE HISTORIES OF NORTH AMERICAN SHORE BIRDS.** Including 81 varieties of such birds as sandpipers, woodcocks, snipes, phalaropes, oyster catchers, and many others. Index for each volume. Bibliographies of 449 entries. 121 full-page plates including over 200 photographs. Total of 860 pp. 5⅜ x 8½.     Vol. I: T933 Paperbound **$2.35**
Vol. II: T934 Paperbound **$2.35**
The set Paperbound **$4.70**

**LIFE HISTORIES OF NORTH AMERICAN WILD FOWL.** Including 73 varieties of ducks, geese, mergansers, swans, etc. Index for each volume. Bibliographies of 268 items. 106 full-page plates containing close to 200 photographs. Total of 685pp. 5⅜ x 8½.
Vol. I: T285 Paperbound **$2.50**
Vol. II: T286 Paperbound **$2.50**
The set Paperbound **$5.00**

**LIFE HISTORIES OF NORTH AMERICAN GULLS AND TERNS.** 50 different varieties of gulls and terns. Index. Bibliography. 93 plates including 149 photographs. xii + 337pp. 5⅜ x 8½.
T1029 Paperbound **$2.75**

**LIFE HISTORIES OF NORTH AMERICAN GALLINACEOUS BIRDS.** Including partridge, quail, grouse, pheasant, pigeons, doves, and others. Index. Bibliography. 93 full-page plates including 170 photographs. xiii + 490pp. 5⅜ x 8½.     **T1028 Paperbound $2.75**

**THE MALAY ARCHIPELAGO, Alfred Russel Wallace.** The record of the explorations (8 years, 14,000 miles) of the Malay Archipelago by a great scientific observer. A contemporary of Darwin, Wallace independently arrived at the concept of evolution by natural selection, applied the new theories of evolution to later genetic discoveries, and made significant contributions to biology, zoology, and botany. This work is still one of the classics of natural history and travel. It contains the author's reports of the different native peoples of the islands, descriptions of the island groupings, his accounts of the animals, birds, and insects that flourished in this area. The reader is carried through strange lands, alien cultures, and new theories, and will share in an exciting, unrivalled travel experience. Unabridged reprint of the 1922 edition, with 62 drawings and maps. 3 appendices, one on cranial measurements. xvii + 515pp. 5⅜ x 8.     **T187 Paperbound $2.00**

**THE TRAVELS OF WILLIAM BARTRAM, edited by Mark Van Doren.** This famous source-book of American anthropology, natural history, geography is the record kept by Bartram in the 1770's, on travels through the wilderness of Florida, Georgia, the Carolinas. Containing accurate and beautiful descriptions of Indians, settlers, fauna, flora, it is one of the finest pieces of Americana ever written. Introduction by Mark Van Doren. 13 original illustrations. Index. 448pp. 5⅜ x 8.     **T13 Paperbound $2.00**

**COMMON SPIDERS OF THE UNITED STATES, J. H. Emerton.** Only non-technical, but thorough, reliable guide to spiders for the layman. Over 200 spiders from all parts of the country, arranged by scientific classification, are identified by shape and color, number of eyes, habitat and range, habits, etc. Full text, 501 line drawings and photographs, and valuable introduction explain webs, poisons, threads, capturing and preserving spiders, etc. Index. New synoptic key by S. W. Frost. xxiv + 225pp. 5⅜ x 8.     **T223 Paperbound $1.45**

# CATALOGUE OF DOVER BOOKS

**LIFE HISTORIES OF NORTH AMERICAN MARSH BIRDS.** A wealth of data on 54 different kinds of marsh bird (flamingo, ibis, bittern, heron, egret, crane, crake, rail, coot, etc.). Index. Bibliography. 98 full-page plates containing 179 black-and-white photographs. xiv + 392pp. 5⅜ x 8½.
T1082 Paperbound **$2.75**

**LIFE HISTORIES OF NORTH AMERICAN DIVING BIRDS.** Thirty-six different diving birds including grebe, loon, auk, murre, puffin, and the like. Index. Bibliography. 55 full-page plates (92 photographs). xiv + 239pp. 5⅜ x 8½.
T1091 Paperbound **$2.75**

**LIFE HISTORIES OF NORTH AMERICAN WOOD WARBLERS.** Covers about 58 types. Index. Bibliography. 83 full-page plates containing 125 black-and-white photographs. xi + 734pp. of text. 5⅜ x 8½.
Vol. I: T1153 Paperbound **$2.50**
Vol. II: T1154 Paperbound **$2.50**
The set Paperbound **$5.00**

**LIFE HISTORIES OF NORTH AMERICAN FLYCATCHERS, LARKS, SWALLOWS, AND THEIR ALLIES.** Complete information on about 78 different varieties. Index. Bibliography. 70 full-page plates (117 photographs). xi + 555pp. of text. 5⅜ x 8½.
T1090 Paperbound **$2.75**

**AMERICAN WILDLIFE, AND PLANTS: A GUIDE TO WILDLIFE FOOD HABITS, A. C. Martin, H. S. Zim, A. L. Nelson.** Result of 75 years of research by U. S. Fish and Wildlife Service into food and feeding habits of more than 1,000 species of birds and mammals, their distribution in America, migratory habits, and the most important plant-animal relationships. Treats over 300 common species of birds, fur and game animals, small mammals, hoofed browsers, fish, amphibians, reptiles by group, giving data on their food, ranges, habits and economies. Also focuses on the different genera of plants that furnish food for our wildlife, animals that use them, and their value. Only thorough study of its kind in existence. "Of immense value to sportsmen, naturalists, bird students, foresters, landscape architects, botanists," NATURE. "Undoubtedly an essential handbook," SCIENTIFIC MONTHLY. Unabridged republication of 1951 edition. Over 600 illustrations, maps, etc. Classified bibliography. Index. x + 500pp. 5⅜ x 8.
T793 Paperbound **$2.25**

**HOW TO KNOW THE WILD FLOWERS, Mrs. Wm. Starr Dana.** A Guide to the names, haunts, and habits of wild flowers. Well-known classic of nature lore. Informative and delightful. Plants classified by color and season of their typical flowers for easy identification. Thorough coverage of more than 1,000 important flowering, berry-bearing and foliage plants of Eastern and Central United States and Canada. Complete botanical information about each important plant. Also history, uses, folklore, habitat, etc. Nomenclature modernized by C. J. Hylander. 174 full-page illustrations by Marion Satterlee. xii + 481pp. 5⅜ x 8½.
T332 Paperbound **$1.85**

**HOW PLANTS GET THEIR NAMES, L. H. Bailey.** Introduction to botanical nomenclature for the horticulturist and garden-lover. Discussions of Carl Linnaeus, "father of botany," and analysis of his definitions of genus and species, a brief history of the science before Linnaean systematization, a chapter on plant identification, a mine of information on the rules of nomenclature and Latin stems and word-endings used in botanical nomenclature, with pronunciation guides. An important section contains a full list of generic terms of horticultural literature and common Latin words and their English botanical applications and meanings. "Written with knowledge and authority, charm and eloquence and poetic imagination on the varied aspects of the author's specialty," New York Times. 11 illustrations. vi + 181pp. 5⅜ x 8½.
T796 Paperbound **$1.25**

**THE CACTACEAE: DESCRIPTIONS AND ILLUSTRATIONS OF PLANTS OF THE CACTUS FAMILY, N. L. Britton and J. N. Rose.** Definitive study of plants of the Cactus Family. The authors devoted more than 15 years of research to this monumental task and produced an exhaustive, rigorously scientific account never likely to be superseded. 3 major classifications, or tribes, are recognized, under which they arrange and describe in full detail 124 genera and 1,235 species of cactus from all over the world. Complete data on each species: leaves, flowers, seeds, fruit, distribution, growth, spines, stem structure, economic uses, etc. In addition, 125 keys facilitate identification of genera and species. For teachers and students of botany and forestry, naturalists, conservationists, and nature lovers, this is an indispensable work. Unabridged republication of second (1937) edition. First edition originally published under the auspices of the Carnegie Institution, Washington, D.C. 4 vols. bound as 2. 1279 illustrations, photographs, sketches, etc. 137 plates. Total of xxvii + 1039pp. 8 x 10¼.
T771 Clothbound, 2-volume set **$20.00**

**GUIDE TO SOUTHERN TREES, Elwood S. and J. George Harrar.** A handy, comprehensive 700-page manual with numerous illustrations and information on more than 350 different kinds of trees, covering the entire area south of the Mason-Dixon line from the Atlantic Ocean to the Florida Keys and western Texas. Descriptions range from the common pine, cypress, walnut, beech, and elm to such rare species as Franklinia, etc. A mine of information on leaves, flowers, twigs, bark, fruit, distribution etc. of each kind of tree. Eminently readable, written in non-technical language, it is an indispensable handbook for all lovers of the outdoors. Revised edition. Index. 81-item bibliography. Glossary. 200 full-page illustrations. ix + 709pp. 4⅝ x 6⅜.
T945 Paperbound **$2.25**

# CATALOGUE OF DOVER BOOKS

**WESTERN FOREST TREES, James B. Berry.** For years a standard guide to the trees of the Western United States. Covers over 70 different subspecies, ranging from the Pacific shores to western South Dakota, New Mexico, etc. Much information on range and distribution, growth habits, appearance, leaves, bark, fruit, twigs, etc. for each tree discussed, plus material on wood of the trees and its uses. Basic division (Trees with needle-like leaves, scale-like leaves, and compound, lobed or divided, and simple broadleaf trees), along with almost 100 illustrations (mostly full-size) of buds, leaves, etc., aids in easy identification of just about any tree of the area. Many subsidiary keys. Revised edition. Introduction. 12 photos. 85 illustrations by Mary E. Eaton. Index. xii + 212pp. 5⅜ x 8.
T1138 Paperbound **$1.35**

**MANUAL OF THE TREES OF NORTH AMERICA (EXCLUSIVE OF MEXICO), Charles Sprague Sargent.** The magnum opus of the greatest American dendrologist. Based on 44 years of original research, this monumental work is still the most comprehensive and reliable sourcebook on the subject. Includes 185 genera and 717 species of trees (and many shrubs) found in the U.S., Canada, and Alaska. 783 illustrative drawings by C. E. Faxon and Mary W. Gill. An all-encompassing lifetime reference book for students, teachers of botany and forestry, naturalists, conservationists, and all nature lovers. Includes an 11-page analytical key to genera to help the beginner locate any tree by its leaf characteristics. Within the text over 100 further keys aid in easy identification. Synopsis of families. Glossary. Index. 783 illustrations, 1 map. Total of 1 + 891pp. 5⅜ x 8.
T277 Vol. I Paperbound **$2.25**
T278 Vol. II Paperbound **$2.25**
The set **$4.50**

**TREES OF THE EASTERN AND CENTRAL UNITED STATES AND CANADA, W. M. Harlow,** Professor of Wood Technology, College of Forestry, State University of N. Y., Syracuse, N. Y. This middle-level text is a serious work covering more than 140 native trees and important escapes, with information on general appearance, growth habit, leaf forms, flowers, fruit, bark, and other features. Commercial use, distribution, habitat, and woodlore are also given. Keys within the text enable you to locate various species with ease. With this book you can identify at sight almost any tree you are likely to encounter; you will know which trees have edible fruit, which are suitable for house planting, and much other useful and interesting information. More than 600 photographs and figures. xiii + 288pp. 4⅝ x 6½.
T395 Paperbound **$1.35**

**FRUIT KEY AND TWIG KEY TO TREES AND SHRUBS (FRUIT KEY TO NORTHEASTERN TREES, TWIG TREE TO DECIDUOUS WOODY PLANTS OF EASTERN NORTH AMERICA), W. M. Harlow.** The only guides with photographs of every twig and fruit described—especially valuable to the novice. The fruit key (both deciduous trees and evergreens) has an introduction explaining seeding, organs involved, fruit types and habits. The twig key introduction treats growth and morphology. In the keys proper, identification is easy and almost automatic. This exceptional work, widely used in university courses, is especially useful for identification in winter, or from the fruit or seed only. Over 350 photos, up to 3 times natural size. Bibliography, glossary, index of common and scientific names, in each key. xvii + 125pp. 5⅝ x 8⅜.
T511 Paperbound **$1.25**

**HOW TO KNOW THE FERNS, F. T. Parsons.** Ferns, among our most lovely native plants, are all too little known. This modern classic of nature lore will enable the layman to identify any American fern he is likely to come across. After an introduction on the structure and life of ferns, the 57 most important ferns are fully pictured and described (arranged upon a simple identification key). Index of Latin and English names. 61 illustrations and 42 full-page plates. xiv + 215pp. 5⅜ x 8.
T740 Paperbound **$1.35**

**OUR SMALL NATIVE ANIMALS: THEIR HABITS AND CARE, R. Snedigar,** Curator of Reptiles, Chicago Zoological Park. An unusual nature handbook containing all the vital facts of habitat, distribution, foods, and special habits in brief life histories of 114 different species of squirrels, chipmunks, rodents, larger mammals, birds, amphibians, lizards and snakes. Liberally sprinkled with first-hand anecdotes. A wealth of information on capturing and caring for these animals: proper pens and cages, correct diet, curing diseases, special equipment required, etc. Addressed to the teacher interested in classroom demonstrations, the camp director, and to anyone who ever wanted a small animal for a pet. Revised edition, New preface. Index. 62 halftones. 14 line drawings. xviii + 296pp. 5⅜ x 8⅛.
T1022 Paperbound **$1.75**

**INSECT LIFE AND INSECT NATURAL HISTORY, S. W. Frost.** Unusual for emphasizing habits, social life, and ecological relations of insects, rather than more academic aspects of classification and morphology. Prof. Frost's enthusiasm and knowledge are everywhere evident as he discusses insect associations, and specialized habits like leaf-mining, leaf-rolling, and case-making, the gall insects, the boring insects, aquatic insects, etc. He examines all sorts of matters not usually covered in general works, such as: insects as human food; insect music and musicians; insect response to electric and radio waves; use of insects in art and literature. The admirably executed purpose of this book, which covers the middle ground between elementary treatment and scholarly monographs, is to excite the reader to observe for himself. Over 700 illustrations. Extensive bibliography. x + 524pp. 5⅜ x 8.
T517 Paperbound **$2.25**

# Biological Sciences

**AN INTRODUCTION TO GENETICS, A. H. Sturtevant and G. W. Beadle.** A very thorough exposition of genetic analysis and the chromosome mechanics of higher organisms by two of the world's most renowned biologists, A. H. Sturtevant, one of the founders of modern genetics, and George Beadle, Nobel laureate in 1958. Does not concentrate on the biochemical approach, but rather more on observed data from experimental evidence and results . . . from Drosophila and other life forms. Some chapter titles: Sex chromosomes; Sex-Linkage; Autosomal Inheritance;; Chromosome Maps; Intra-Chromosomal Rearrangements; Inversions—and Incomplete Chromosomes; Translocations; Lethals; Mutations; Heterogeneous Populations; Genes and Phenotypes; The Determination and Differentiation of Sex; etc. Slightly corrected reprint of 1939 edition. New preface by Drs. Sturtevant and Beadle. 1 color plate. 126 figures. Bibliographies. Index. 391pp. 5⅜ x 8½. S306 Paperbound **$2.00**

**THE GENETICAL THEORY OF NATURAL SELECTION, R. A. Fisher.** 2nd revised edition of a vital reviewing of Darwin's Selection Theory in terms of particulate inheritance, by one of the great authorities on experimental and theoretical genetics. Theory is stated in mathematical form. Special features of particulate inheritance are examined: evolution of dominance, maintenance of specific variability, mimicry and sexual selection, etc. 5 chapters on man and his special circumstances as a social animal. 16 photographs. Bibliography. Index. x + 310pp. 5⅜ x 8. S466 Paperbound **$2.00**

**THE ORIENTATION OF ANIMALS: KINESES, TAXES AND COMPASS REACTIONS, Gottfried S. Fraenkel and Donald L. Gunn.** A basic work in the field of animal orientations. Complete, detailed survey of everything known in the subject up to 1940s, enlarged and revised to cover major developments to 1960. Analyses of simpler types of orientation are presented in Part I: kinesis, klinotaxis, tropotaxis, telotaxis, etc. Part II covers more complex reactions originating from temperature changes, gravity, chemical stimulation, etc. The twolight experiment and unilateral blinding are dealt with, as is the problem of determinism or volition in lower animals. The book has become the universally-accepted guide to all who deal with the subject—zoologists, biologists, psychologists, and the like. Second, enlarged edition, revised to 1960. Bibliography of over 500 items. 135 illustrations. Indices. xiii + 376pp. 5⅜ x 8½. T786 Paperbound **$2.25**

**THE BEHAVIOUR AND SOCIAL LIFE OF HONEYBEES, C. R. Ribbands.** Definitive survey of all aspects of honeybee life and behavior; completely scientific in approach, but written in interesting, everyday language that both professionals and laymen will appreciate. Basic coverage of physiology, anatomy, sensory equipment; thorough account of honeybee behavior in the field (foraging activities, nectar and pollen gathering, how individuals find their way home and back to food areas, mating habits, etc.); details of communication in various field and hive situations. An extensive treatment of activities within the hive community—food sharing, wax production, comb building, swarming, the queen, her life and relationship with the workers, etc. A must for the beekeeper, natural historian, biologist, entomologist, social scientist, et al. "An indispensable reference," J. Hambleton, BᴋES. "Recommended in the strongest of terms," AMERICAN SCIENTIST. 9 plates. 66 figures. Indices. 693-item bibliography. 252pp. 5⅜ x 8½. T1137 Paperbound **$2.00**

**BIRD DISPLAY: AN INTRODUCTION TO THE STUDY OF BIRD PSYCHOLOGY, E. A. Armstrong.** The standard work on bird display, based on extensive observation by the author and reports of other observers. This important contribution to comparative psychology covers the behavior and ceremonial rituals of hundreds of birds from gannet and heron to birds of paradise and king penguins. Chapters discuss such topics as the ceremonial of the gannet, ceremonial gaping, disablement reactions, the expression of emotions, the evolution and function of social ceremonies, social hierarchy in bird life, dances of birds and men, songs, etc. Free of technical terminology, this work will be equally interesting to psychologists and zoologists as well as bird lovers of all backgrounds. 32 photographic plates. New introduction by the author. List of scientific names of birds. Bibliography. 3-part index. 431pp. 5⅜ x 8½. T1128 Paperbound **$2.00**

**THE SPECIFICITY OF SEROLOGICAL REACTIONS, Karl Landsteiner.** With a Chapter on Molecular Structure and Intermolecular Forces by Linus Pauling. Dr. Landsteiner, winner of the Nobel Prize in 1930 for the discovery of the human blood groups, devoted his life to fundamental research and played a leading role in the development of immunology. This authoritative study is an account of the experiments he and his colleagues carried out on antigens and serological reactions with simple compounds. Comprehensive coverage of the basic concepts of immunology includes such topics as: The Serological Specificity of Proteins, Antigens, Antibodies, Artificially Conjugated Antigens, Non-Protein Cell Substances such as polysaccharides, etc., Antigen-Antibody Reactions (Toxin Neutralization, Precipitin Reactions, Agglutination, etc.). Discussions of toxins, bacterial proteins, viruses, hormones, enzymes, etc. in the context of immunological phenomena. New introduction by Dr. Merrill Chase of the Rockefeller Institute. Extensive bibliography and bibliography of author's writings. Index. xviii + 330pp. 5⅜ x 8½. S299 Paperbound **$2.00**

# CATALOGUE OF DOVER BOOKS

**CULTURE METHODS FOR INVERTEBRATE ANIMALS, P. S. Galtsoff, F. E. Lutz, P. S. Welch, J. G. Needham, eds.** A compendium of practical experience of hundreds of scientists and technicians, covering invertebrates from protozoa to chordata, in 313 articles on 17 phyla. Explains in great detail food, protection, environment, reproduction conditions, rearing methods, embryology, breeding seasons, schedule of development, much more. Includes at least one species of each considerable group. Half the articles are on class insecta. Introduction. 97 illustrations. Bibliography. Index. xxix + 590pp. 5⅜ x 8. S526 Paperbound **$2.75**

**THE BIOLOGY OF THE LABORATORY MOUSE, edited by G. D. Snell.** 1st prepared in 1941 by the staff of the Roscoe B. Jackson Memorial Laboratory, this is still the standard treatise on the mouse, assembling an enormous amount of material for which otherwise you spend hours of research. Embryology, reproduction, histology, spontaneous tumor formation, genetics of tumor transplantation, endocrine secretion & tumor formation, milk, influence & tumor formation, inbred, hybrid animals, parasites, infectious diseases, care & recording. Classified bibliography of 1122 items. 172 figures, including 128 photos. ix + 497pp. 6⅛ x 9¼. S248 Clothbound **$6.00**

**MATHEMATICAL BIOPHYSICS: PHYSICO-MATHEMATICAL FOUNDATIONS OF BIOLOGY, N. Rashevsky.** One of most important books in modern biology, now revised, expanded with new chapters, to include most significant recent contributions. Vol. 1: Diffusion phenomena, particularly diffusion drag forces, their effects. Old theory of cell division based on diffusion drag forces, other theoretical approaches, more exhaustively treated than ever. Theories of excitation, conduction in nerves, with formal theories plus physico-chemical theory. Vol. 2: Mathematical theories of various phenomena in central nervous system. New chapters on theory of color vision, of random nets. Principle of optimal design, extended from earlier edition. Principle of relational mapping of organisms, numerous applications. Introduces into mathematical biology such branches of math as topology, theory of sets. Index. 236 illustrations. Total of 988pp. 5⅜ x 8. S574 Vol. 1 (Books 1, 2) Paperbound **$2.50**
S575 Vol. 2 (Books 3, 4) Paperbound **$2.50**
2 vol. set **$5.00**

**ELEMENTS OF MATHEMATICAL BIOLOGY, A. J. Lotka.** A pioneer classic, the first major attempt to apply modern mathematical techniques on a large scale to phenomena of biology, biochemistry, psychology, ecology, similar life sciences. Partial Contents: Statistical meaning of irreversibility; Evolution as redistribution; Equations of kinetics of evolving systems; Chemical, inter-species equilibrium; parameters of state; Energy transformers of nature, etc. Can be read with profit even by those having no advanced math; unsurpassed as study-reference. Formerly titled ELEMENTS OF PHYSICAL BIOLOGY. 72 figures. xxx + 460pp. 5⅜ x 8. S346 Paperbound **$2.45**

**THE BIOLOGY OF THE AMPHIBIA, G. K. Noble,** Late Curator of Herpetology at the Am. Mus. of Nat. Hist. Probably the most used text on amphibia, unmatched in comprehensiveness, clarity, detail. 19 chapters plus 85-page supplement cover development; heredity; life history; speciation; adaptation; sex, integument, respiratory, circulatory, digestive, muscular, nervous systems; instinct, intelligence, habits, environment, economic value, relationships, classification, etc. "Nothing comparable to it," C. H. Pope, Curator of Amphibia, Chicago Mus. of Nat. Hist. 1047 bibliographic references. 174 illustrations. 600pp. 5⅜ x 8. S206 Paperbound **$2.98**

**STUDIES ON THE STRUCTURE AND DEVELOPMENT OF VERTEBRATES, E. S. Goodrich.** A definitive study by the greatest modern comparative anatomist. Exceptional in its accounts of the ossicles of the ear, the separate divisions of the coelom and mammalian diaphragm, and the 5 chapters devoted to the head region. Also exhaustive morphological and phylogenetic expositions of skeleton, fins and limbs, skeletal visceral arches and labial cartilages, visceral clefts and gills, vacular, respiratory, excretory, and peripheral nervous systems, etc., from fish to the higher mammals. 754 illustrations. 69 page biographical study by C. C. Hardy. Bibliography of 1186 references. "What an undertaking . . . to write a textbook which will summarize adequately and succinctly all that has been done in the realm of Vertebrate Morphology these recent years," Journal of Anatomy. Index. Two volumes. Total 906pp. 5⅜ x 8. Two vol. set S449-50 Paperbound **$5.00**

**A TREATISE ON PHYSIOLOGICAL OPTICS, H. von Helmholtz,** Ed. by J. P. C. Southall. Unmatched for thoroughness, soundness, and comprehensiveness, this is still the most important work ever produced in the field of physiological optics. Revised and annotated, it contains everything known about the subject up to 1925. Beginning with a careful anatomical description of the eye, the main body of the text is divided into three general categories: The Dioptrics of the Eye (covering optical imagery, blur circles on the retina, the mechanism of accommodation, chromatic aberration, etc.); The Sensations of Vision (including stimulation of the organ of vision, simple and compound colors, the intensity and duration of light, variations of sensitivity, contrast, etc.); and The Perceptions of Vision (containing movements of the eyes, the monocular field of vision, direction, perception of depth, binocular double vision, etc.). Appendices cover later findings on optical imagery, refraction, ophthalmoscopy, and many other matters. Unabridged, corrected republication of the original English translation of the third German edition. 3 volumes bound as 2. Complete bibliography, 1911-1925. Indices. 312 illustrations. 6 full-page plates, 3 in color. Total of 1,749pp. 5⅜ x 8. Two-volume set S15, 16 Clothbound **$15.00**

# Philosophy, Religion

**GUIDE TO PHILOSOPHY, C. E. M. Joad.** A modern classic which examines many crucial problems which man has pondered through the ages: Does free will exist? Is there plan in the universe? How do we know and validate our knowledge? Such opposed solutions as subjective idealism and realism, chance and teleology, vitalism and logical positivism, are evaluated and the contributions of the great philosophers from the Greeks to moderns like Russell, Whitehead, and others, are considered in the context of each problem. "The finest introduction," BOSTON TRANSCRIPT. Index. Classified bibliography. 592pp. 5⅜ x 8.
T297 Paperbound **$2.00**

**HISTORY OF ANCIENT PHILOSOPHY, W. Windelband.** One of the clearest, most accurate comprehensive surveys of Greek and Roman philosophy. Discusses ancient philosophy in general, intellectual life in Greece in the 7th and 6th centuries B.C., Thales, Anaximander, Anaximenes, Heraclitus, the Eleatics, Empedocles, Anaxagoras, Leucippus, the Pythagoreans, the Sophists, Socrates, Democritus (20 pages), Plato (50 pages), Aristotle (70 pages), the Peripatetics, Stoics, Epicureans, Sceptics, Neo-platonists, Christian Apologists, etc. 2nd German edition translated by H. E. Cushman. xv + 393pp. 5⅜ x 8.
T357 Paperbound **$1.85**

**ILLUSTRATIONS OF THE HISTORY OF MEDIEVAL THOUGHT AND LEARNING, R. L. Poole.** Basic analysis of the thought and lives of the leading philosophers and ecclesiastics from the 8th to the 14th century—Abailard, Ockham, Wycliffe, Marsiglio of Padua, and many other great thinkers who carried the torch of Western culture and learning through the "Dark Ages": political, religious, and metaphysical views. Long a standard work for scholars and one of the best introductions to medieval thought for beginners. Index. 10 Appendices. xiii + 327pp. 5⅜ x 8.
T674 Paperbound **$1.85**

**PHILOSOPHY AND CIVILIZATION IN THE MIDDLE AGES, M. de Wulf.** This semi-popular survey covers aspects of medieval intellectual life such as religion, philosophy, science, the arts, etc. It also covers feudalism vs. Catholicism, rise of the universities, mendicant orders, monastic centers, and similar topics. Unabridged. Bibliography. Index. viii + 320pp. 5⅜ x 8.
T284 Paperbound **$1.85**

**AN INTRODUCTION TO SCHOLASTIC PHILOSOPHY, Prof. M. de Wulf.** Formerly entitled SCHOLASTICISM OLD AND NEW, this volume examines the central scholastic tradition from St. Anselm, Albertus Magnus, Thomas Aquinas, up to Suarez in the 17th century. The relation of scholasticism to ancient and medieval philosophy and science in general is clear and easily followed. The second part of the book considers the modern revival of scholasticism, the Louvain position, relations with Kantianism and Positivism. Unabridged. xvi + 271pp. 5⅜ x 8.
T296 Clothbound **$3.50**
T283 Paperbound **$1.75**

**A HISTORY OF MODERN PHILOSOPHY, H. Höffding.** An exceptionally clear and detailed coverage of western philosophy from the Renaissance to the end of the 19th century. Major and minor men such as Pomponazzi, Bodin, Boehme, Telesius, Bruno, Copernicus, da Vinci, Kepler, Galileo, Bacon, Descartes, Hobbes, Spinoza, Leibniz, Wolff, Locke, Newton, Berkeley, Hume, Erasmus, Montesquieu, Voltaire, Diderot, Rousseau, Lessing, Kant, Herder, Fichte, Schelling, Hegel, Schopenhauer, Comte, Mill, Darwin, Spencer, Hartmann, Lange, and many others, are discussed in terms of theory of knowledge, logic, cosmology, and psychology. Index. 2 volumes, total of 1159pp. 5⅜ x 8.
T117 Vol. 1, Paperbound **$2.25**
T118 Vol. 2, Paperbound **$2.25**

**ARISTOTLE, A. E. Taylor.** A brilliant, searching non-technical account of Aristotle and his thought written by a foremost Platonist. It covers the life and works of Aristotle; classification of the sciences; logic; first philosophy; matter and form; causes; motion and eternity; God; physics; metaphysics; and similar topics. Bibliography. New Index compiled for this edition. 128pp. 5⅜ x 8.
T280 Paperbound **$1.00**

**THE SYSTEM OF THOMAS AQUINAS, M. de Wulf.** Leading Neo-Thomist, one of founders of University of Louvain, gives concise exposition to central doctrines of Aquinas, as a means toward determining his value to modern philosophy, religion. Formerly "Medieval Philosophy Illustrated from the System of Thomas Aquinas." Trans. by E. Messenger. Introduction. 151pp. 5⅜ x 8.
T568 Paperbound **$1.25**

**LEIBNIZ, H. W. Carr.** Most stimulating middle-level coverage of basic philosophical thought of Leibniz. Easily understood discussion, analysis of major works: "Theodicy," "Principles of Nature and Grace," "Monadology"; Leibniz's influence; intellectual growth; correspondence; disputes with Bayle, Malebranche, Newton; importance of his thought today, with reinterpretation in modern terminology. "Power and mastery," London Times. Bibliography. Index. 226pp. 5⅜ x 8.
T624 Paperbound **$1.35**

# History, Political Science

**THE POLITICAL THOUGHT OF PLATO AND ARISTOTLE, E. Barker.** One of the clearest and most accurate expositions of the corpus of Greek political thought. This standard source contains exhaustive analyses of the "Republic" and other Platonic dialogues and Aristotle's "Politics" and "Ethics," and discusses the origin of these ideas in Greece, contributions of other Greek theorists, and modifications of Greek ideas by thinkers from Aquinas to Hegel. "Must" reading for anyone interested in the history of Western thought. Index. Chronological Table of Events. 2 Appendixes. xxiv + 560pp. 5⅜ x 8. T521 Paperbound **$1.85**

**THE IDEA OF PROGRESS, J. B. Bury.** Practically unknown before the Reformation, the idea of progress has since become one of the central concepts of western civilization. Prof. Bury analyzes its evolution in the thought of Greece, Rome, the Middle Ages, the Renaissance, to its flowering in all branches of science, religion, philosophy, industry, art, and literature, during and following the 16th century. Introduction by Charles Beard. Index. xl + 357pp. 5⅜ x 8. T40 Paperbound **$2.00**

**THE ANCIENT GREEK HISTORIANS, J. B. Bury.** This well known, easily read work covers the entire field of classical historians from the early writers to Herodotus, Thucydides, Xenophon, through Poseidonius and such Romans as Tacitus, Cato, Caesar, Livy. Scores of writers are studied biographically, in style, sources, accuracy, structure, historical concepts, and influences. Recent discoveries such as the Oxyrhinchus papyri are referred to, as well as such great scholars as Nissen, Gomperz, Cornford, etc. "Totally unblemished by pedantry." Outlook. "The best account in English," Dutcher, A Guide to Historical Lit. Bibliography, Index. x + 281pp. 5⅜ x 8. T397 Paperbound **$1.65**

**HISTORY OF THE LATER ROMAN EMPIRE, J. B. Bury.** This standard work by the leading Byzantine scholar of our time discusses the later Roman and early Byzantine empires from 395 A.D. through the death of Justinian in 565, in their political, social, cultural, theological, and military aspects. Contemporary documents are quoted in full, making this the most complete reconstruction of the period and a fit successor to Gibbon's "Decline and Fall." "Most unlikely that it will ever be superseded," Glanville Downey, Dumbarton Oaks Research Lib. Geneological tables. 5 maps. Bibliography. Index. 2 volumes total of 965pp. 5⅜ x 8. T398, 399 Two volume set, Paperbound **$4.00**

**A HISTORY OF ANCIENT GEOGRAPHY, E. H. Bunbury.** Standard study, in English, of ancient geography; never equalled for scope, detail. First full account of history of geography from Greeks' first world picture based on mariners, through Ptolemy. Discusses every important map, discovery, figure, travel expedition, war, conjecture, narrative, bearing on subject. Chapters on Homeric geography, Herodotus, Alexander expedition, Strabo, Pliny, Ptolemy, would stand alone as exhaustive monographs. Includes minor geographers, men not usually regarded in this context: Hecataeus, Pytheas, Hipparchus, Artemidorus, Marinus of Tyre, etc. Uses information gleaned from military campaigns such as Punic Wars, Hannibal's passage of Alps, campaigns of Lucullus, Pompey, Caesar's wars, the Trojan War. New introduction by W. H. Stahl, Brooklyn College. Bibliography. Index. 20 maps. 1426pp. 5⅜ x 8. T570-1, clothbound, 2-volume set **$12.50**

**POLITICAL PARTIES, Robert Michels.** Classic of social science, reference point for all later work, deals with nature of leadership in social organization on government and trade union levels. Probing tendency of oligarchy to replace democracy, it studies need for leadership, desire for organization, psychological motivations, vested interests, hero worship, reaction of leaders to power, press relations, many other aspects. Trans. by E. & C. Paul. Introduction. 447pp. 5⅜ x 8. T569 Paperbound **$2.00**

**A HISTORY OF HISTORICAL WRITING, Harry Elmer Barnes.** Virtually the only adequate survey of the whole course of historical writing in a single volume. Surveys developments from the beginnings of historiographies in the ancient Near East and the Classical World, up through the Cold War. Covers major historians in detail, shows interrelationship with cultural background, makes clear individual contributions, evaluates and estimates importance; also enormously rich upon minor authors and thinkers who are usually passed over. Packed with scholarship and learning, clear, easily written. Indispensable to every student of history. Revised and enlarged up to 1961. Index and bibliography. xv + 442pp. 5⅜ x 8½. T104 Paperbound **$2.25**

*Prices subject to change without notice.*

*Dover publishes books on art, music, philosophy, literature, languages, history, social sciences, psychology, handcrafts, orientalia, puzzles and entertainments, chess, pets and gardens, books explaining science, intermediate and higher mathematics, mathematical physics, engineering, biological sciences, earth sciences, classics of science, etc. Write to:*

Dept. catrr.
Dover Publications, Inc.
180 Varick Street, N. Y. 14, N. Y.